D0984466

The Last American CEO

Jason Vines
&
Joe Cappy

Published by Waldorf Publishing
2140 Hall Johnson Road
#102-345
Grapevine, Texas 76051
www.WaldorfPublishing.com

The Last American CEO

ISBN: 978-1-944245-10-8
Library of Congress Control Number: 2015957010

Copyright © 2016

All rights reserved. No part of this book may be reproduced
or transmitted in any form or by any means whatsoever
without express written permission from the author, except
in the case of brief quotations embodied in critical articles
and reviews. Please refer all pertinent questions to the
publisher. All rights reserved. No part of this book may
be reproduced or transmitted in any form or by any means,
electronic or mechanical, including photocopying,
recording, or by an information storage and retrieval
system except by a reviewer who may quote brief passages
in a review to be printed in a magazine or newspaper
without permission in writing from the publisher.

Dedication

This book is dedicated in memory to our late parents
George and Antonetta Mele Capizzi and Cecil Vines and to
Carol Cappy who shared these turbulent times with her
partner Joe Cappy until her untimely death in January
1989...And to Peggy Vines.

Table of Contents

Introduction by Jason Vines

In December 2014, just a month after my first book launched, I got a call from an old friend. Check that: not just an old friend, but probably the greatest influence on my career; maybe my life, other than my wife and my parents.

Joe Cappy was on the line. Cappy, the last CEO of American Motors before Chrysler Corporation acquired it in 1987, had just read my book, ***What Did Jesus Drive? Crisis PR in Cars, Computers and Christianity,*** and he was now apparently "inspired" to tell his story in the rough-and-tumble world of the global automotive industry.

"Would you help me?" he asked. How could I say no; I owed my career to the man.

I was 29 years old, a kid from a small town in Iowa, then a father of two and being groomed by Cappy to move into his marketing organization for the Jeep/Eagle Division of Chrysler Corporation. The Friday before the Monday I was to join his team, I got a call from the second in command of Chrysler PR, Steve Harris. "Hey, we just fired the Eagle PR guy and Joe Cappy is wondering if you can take the job?"

PR, Marketing, what's the difference? Oh crap, I would soon learn, but I didn't care at the moment; I just wanted to work with Joe.

And so it began.

Cappy sent me what he had already written, but I knew we needed more. I traveled to his "up-north" home in Northern Michigan and over 24 hours and a round of golf the story came together. Simply put, this book contains it all: the lives and livelihoods of thousands of families on the line, sex, lies, international intrigue, conflicts of interest... and an assassination that almost altered business history. No kidding.

This book was written to be informative and entertaining, as well as to demonstrate how business situations are impacted by rational and irrational human behavior – and conditions beyond anyone's control. It confirms there are many instances where business decisions completely change the course of a company's future.

American Motors Corporation (AMC) is a prime example – from its inception, to its demise as a stand-alone American automotive company through investments by Renault of France, to its acquisition by Chrysler Corporation.

AMC was created to keep several smaller independent automotive companies from fading away into history, like an old soldier, never to be seen again. A birthing merger took place on May 1, 1954, between Nash Motors and Hudson Motor Company, forming a new company named American Motors Corporation.

During its life span, AMC became labeled with more adjectives than one can count – words like struggling, ailing, distressed, poor, failing, damaged, weak, declining, sinking, deteriorating, fading, languishing, wasting, and so on. I think you get the idea.

Somehow, American Motors managed to carry-on in the automotive industry thanks to early leaders like Charles Nash, George Mason, George Romney, and Roy Chapin, Jr.

In 1978, then-Chairman and CEO Gerald Meyers implemented a strategy that involved a French connection. The long-range plan was to have AMC concentrate on its Jeep products, while Renault would be responsible for car products derived from Renault's European passenger car lines to be built in North America and also be imported from Europe. This strategy was rational and financially sound, provided each company produced competitive products for the U.S. automotive industry.

However, both AMC and Renault were experiencing difficult financial times as their products and the markets were changing. What happened next is where this book provides an unfettered insider's view of Chrysler's acquisition of AMC, the turmoil that ensued, and how assassins' bullets quite possibly saved the deal.

Chapter 1
The End of the Beginning

On November 17, 1986, Georges Besse, French automaker Renault's Chairman, was finishing up some last minute business in his office in the Renault headquarters in the western section of Paris. It was time to wrap up and head for home.

It had been a very difficult eighteen months for the 58-year-old leader of French industry, since he had been summoned by the French government to replace the popular Bernard Hanon, who had run the largest French automaker under some difficult times.

Renault had been losing large amounts of money in Europe, while financially supporting a joint venture with the smallest of the U. S. automakers, American Motors Corporation (AMC), in which it owned 46.1 percent. Renault was known as a "Crown Corporation," one owned by the French government. Therefore, the government and its citizens were actually underwriting Renault and AMC's significant losses – a very sensitive and explosive situation when working with a strong labor union in a socialist society.

Georges Besse had an outstanding reputation of leadership and success in many of France's largest and most important industries. This reputation and performance allowed him more flexibility in his dealings with the government.

Besse was at the zenith of his professional career. An educated engineer, he had graduated second in his class at the esteemed Ecole Polytechnique, and went on to the prestigious Ecole de Mines, where he was fifth in his class. This education path was the entryway to the top of France's major state-owned industries.

A peer of Georges Besse described him as "a man of granite, with a dense core, high values, intelligence and sound judgment." The French government believed a change in Renault's leadership was necessary and agreed, despite no actual automotive experience, Besse was the right man for the job.

Upon accepting the position, Besse was told to minimize the funds to the Americans, right-size Renault, and stop the bleeding.

During the next eighteen months, he laid off 21,000 French workers and was bringing the company back into profitability. He did not, however, pull out of the AMC venture despite heavy pressure from the government's treasurer to do so. The labor union unrest boiled over with the loss of union worker jobs, while Renault was still financing AMC in the United States.

Besse believed, as did his predecessor Hanon, that Renault needed to participate in the U.S. market, the largest in the world, if Renault was to remain one of the world's major automotive producers. Renault lacked an adequate dealer network across the pond that AMC provided. He also strongly believed the new Jeep products underway at AMC would be a prime factor in improving AMC's profitability in the U.S and obviously Renault's bottom line back home. Yet, his mind was still open if conditions changed.

Georges Besse was chauffeured to work and home each morning and evening, which allowed him time to read materials he couldn't get to at the office. He lived on Boulevard Edgar-Quinet, in the 14th *arrondissement* in Paris, an area of row houses.

On the evening of November 17, 1986, one of his daughters was looking out of an upstairs window awaiting his arrival at 8:30 p.m., his normal time.

As his car was pulling up in front of his house, two women with a baby carriage were approaching on the sidewalk. Besse was exiting the car, when the women and the carriage stopped and they appeared to be arranging a blanket on an infant. Instead, they pulled out two weapons and one of the women fired into Georges Besse's chest and followed up with a shot point-blank to his face as he crumbled to the sidewalk, fatally wounded. The other woman acted as a backup. They then dropped their weapons and ran to the corner of the block where they were picked up by two men on motorcycles, fleeing the scene of the murder.

While his daughter continued to scream, Georges Besse lay dead on the sidewalk.

Arrested for the assassination in February 1987 were two women and two men who were part of Action Directe, aka Red Army Faction, a militant group of anarchists who had assassinated other European industry leaders for being "imperial capitalists." The killers, Nathalie Menigon and Joelle Aubron, along with their getaway men, Jean-Marc Rouillan and Georges Cipriani, were all convicted and sentenced to life in prison.

Not known publicly at the time, however, was how Georges Besse's death would result in American Motors' final brush with death. It really was, "the end of the beginning."

Chapter 2
Yogi Berra Was Right

The late Hall of Famer and infamous sage reportedly once remarked, "You don't know, what you don't know." And AMC's management, under incredible pressure due to their shaky financial situation, didn't know what Renault and America's number three automaker, Chrysler Corporation, were up to – at least officially from Renault.

AMC was extremely stretched out building a new assembly plant in Bramalea, Ontario, Canada, for an all-new passenger car called the Renault Premier. At the same time, AMC was struggling to become profitable after decades of losses.

What wasn't known was Renault, AMC's 46.1 percent owner, had been in secret contact and discussions with superstar CEO Lee Iacocca and his Chrysler Corporation. These talks, while ongoing over many months, were not moving along in a steady manner. The Renault Chairman, Georges Besse, was willing to listen, but was not convinced the sale of AMC was in the best interest of Renault despite growing pressure from the French government to dump America's weakest automaker.

For Chrysler Corporation, however, and Iacocca, it would be a brilliant strategic move after its own near-death experience years earlier, which included the U.S. government financially backing the automaker as it danced with bankruptcy, as future events subsequently proved. The AMC acquisition would enable Chrysler to avoid a second exposure to bankruptcy in 1989-90, when Jeep products produced top-line revenue and profits, which when combined with profits from Chrysler's ground-breaking minivans profit, kept the company solvent.

As it later turned out, the AMC acquisition also served as the impetus and organizational model for Chrysler to switch its engineering organization to product development "platform teams" already in place at Jeep engineering. Chrysler's Executive Vice President, Bob Lutz, quickly understood the value of this type of organization at Chrysler with its entrenched, and no longer efficient long-time silos, separated by function.

AMC had just regained profitability in the fourth quarter of 1986, after five out of seven years of significant losses. But its biggest weakness was apparent: the lack of capital for long-term product investments. For Renault Chairman Besse, it would be politically expedient to allow Chrysler to take AMC off the French automaker's hands. But political issues did not easily sway him.

After months of discussion and offers by Chrysler, Besse broke off talks with Chrysler in November 1986, as he wanted time to think further about whether or not he should sell Renault's interest in AMC. Despite the political pressure, all indications were showing AMC was turning the corner on profitability and would provide a strong base in the important U.S. market for Renault to expand and be a true global player.

A few short days after the talks were discontinued, Georges Besse was assassinated by the cowardly terrorists as his daughter watched. He was given a State funeral with full French government honors, equal to a head of state, or major military hero. Besse was dead, and so too perhaps was a deal with Chrysler, as well as the long-term viability of American Motors.

Enter Joe Cappy.

Chapter 3
Joe Cappy: "The Mayor of Wisconsin Dells"

Joe Capizzi was born May 13, 1934, in Chicago,
Illinois to George and Antonetta Mele Capizzi. George
worked as a store superintendent – basically the head of
operations – for several large department store chains in
Chicago, and then moved the family to Wisconsin Dells,
Wisconsin, where he bought out a small department store to
make it his own – Cappy's Department Store. George
changed his name to Cappy for business purposes, but not
legally. He bought all the crappy merchandise that came
with the store and sold it in a fire sale – like five pairs of
ladies patent leather button shoes for a buck – in order to
bring in modern merchandise.

As a teen, Joe worked in his dad's store, sold tourists
postcards on a river cruise and ran the concession stand at
the local semi-pro baseball park – often all three on the
same day in the summer. One Sunday morning, two fair-
skinned Chicago men and their wives bought caps from
him at the department store to protect them from the
blazing sun before taking the river cruise. One of the boat
stops was Coldwater Canyon where Joe was a guide selling
post cards as tourists left the boat to walk through the
canyon. Later that afternoon, one of the boats discharged
the same two couples who had bought the caps earlier.
They joked when they ran into Joe, but Joe ended up selling

them post cards as well. That night, Joe was cooking hot dogs, popping corn, and setting up the concession stand at the ball park where the City team was preparing for a night game.

Lo and behold, the same two men approached the concession stand to buy some refreshments. They were amazed, and exclaimed, "Are you the Mayor as well?"

Cappy graduated from the University of Wisconsin-Madison in June 1956 with degrees in Accounting and Marketing, a wife Carol, and a new baby. The next month he joined Ford Motor Company after interviewing and receiving job offers at General Motors and two retail department chains. He began his career as a $400-a-month accountant in Ford's Special Products Division. He left his young family temporarily to start his job in Dearborn, Michigan, just outside of Detroit, and rented a cheap room in downtown Detroit after asking his dad where he should stay. "The YMCA of course!" (Within a day, the Ford personnel department told him to get a real motel room along a major corridor in Dearborn, Telegraph Road.) If it was "fun" to stay at the YMCA in the mid-1950s, Cappy did so for only a few days.

Inside the "Specials Products Division" at Ford, Cappy worked in a bullpen alongside other accountants. With no family to go home to after normal hours, Joe always stayed late, pouring over Ford's notorious Accounting Manuals – literally 18 inches of three-ring binders. "Joe, it's five o' clock. Time to go!" "Nope, I need to know this stuff." His manager, Jim Stead, would stick around and they would talk after hours.

After six months at Ford, Cappy was called up for active duty in the U.S. Army, a commitment he made while in ROTC at University of Wisconsin. But before he shipped off to Fort Eustis, Virginia, for service, he wanted to see the "special product" for which he had been crunching numbers but had not seen, code-named the "E-Car." Joe grabbed Ford PR guy C. Gayle Warnock and asked, "Can I see the car before I leave?" Warnock grabbed Cappy's arm and they headed off to the "E-car's" chief product planner's office, and after entering, had the door locked behind them. (Interesting note: Warnock would write two books about the car's failure.)

The product planner, showing more caution than a CIA operative in the Soviet Union, went to his safe and removed a "top secret" three-ring binder. He explained the competitive advantages of the "E-Car," bragged about what a wild success it was going to be for Ford and then opened the binder, exposing a straight on shot of the car's front end. The "E-car" was the infamous Edsel. Cappy looked on in horror. "The grill of the car looked like a cross between a toilet seat and a vagina!" he thought. "Isn't that wonderful?" the proud papa product planner asked Cappy. "What could I say?" Cappy thought. "No! Your baby looks like a monkey?" Cappy had been reading all kinds of phenomenal preview media and marketing plans for the car in the months since he had joined Ford. "I was completely underwhelmed," he would later remark.

Joe was finally joined by his wife and child at his military stint in Warwick, Virginia, and throughout his time there, his buddies at Ford kept sending him great news clips about the Edsel. In the fall of '57, Ford Motor Company officially launched the Edsel, named after founder Henry Ford's only son and almost instantaneously, it became the biggest flop in the history of the American auto industry. When Cappy returned to Dearborn, his active military commitment over, "Everybody inside the Special Products Division, now renamed the Edsel Division, was in agony," Joe later shared. "The only real bomb I saw in 1957, including six months on a U.S. Army base, was the Edsel."

The 23-year-old's career continued in the Dealer Audit Department of the Mercury, Edsel, and Lincoln (MEL) Division where as a junior auditor he was assigned to visit the company's car dealers and look at their balance sheets and warranty and incentive numbers. What the young Cappy soon found was warranty costs – repaid to the dealers – and vehicle sales incentives were both soaring. Cappy's analysis soon caught the eye of Assistant Controller Austin Schimmel, who concluded "they (the dealers) are screwing us." When Schimmel walked into the Audit Department looking for Cappy's boss, who was vacationing, Joe didn't let Schimmel's interest in his work go to waste. "Austin, we can concentrate on warranty and vehicle sales incentive audits in our computer system (giant computers back in the day would most likely equate to laptop computing prowess today) and do an analysis of the high costs and out-of-line dealer suspects."

Cappy could see Schimmel's brain spinning. "Joe, I'm meeting with my boss tomorrow morning at 9 a.m. and I need to explain how to do this, including the potential recovery of funds taken from us improperly by our dealers."

Working through the night, Cappy mapped out a plan in his office cubicle and later at home, but not before telling his boss's secretary she would need to come into the office extra early to type whatever Cappy would develop. (Sorry, in the man's auto industry of the late 1950s – which was the way the world worked – men somewhat "thought" and women "typed".) Bright and early she met Joe at her desk and within an hour was finished. Cappy scooted over to the Assistant Controller's office and handed Schimmel his work. Schimmel read the plan. "Who did this?" he asked Cappy, still a very junior member of the Ford team. "Ah, I did," said Cappy. "Oh my God. Joe, I meet my boss at 9. You come by his office at 9:15."

Forty five minutes later, a year out of college, Joe Cappy was standing outside the office of one of Ford's most powerful young executives, John Nevin. Schimmel had shared Cappy's plan, and in a sign of true class, wanted the author of the plan to get the credit. The "big guy" shook Cappy's hand and said, "Put this in action as soon as possible." Seemingly, overnight, millions of dollars were recovered.

But Cappy's plan didn't just bust dealers acting badly. He noticed a Long Island N.Y. dealership was doing 100 times the warranty repairs than the average dealers on a specific, mostly labor repair that required prior factory approval. Cappy also noted that sprinkled regularly throughout the dealer's cash parts receipts were the initials "E" and "C." When he confronted the dealership's service and parts managers, he asked them what "E.C." stood for. "Extra Cash," came back the response. Yeah, 50 bucks extra cash here, 100 bucks extra cash there, eventually adding up to big money. But it was all legit, right? The parts manager and service manager explained that from time-to-time, they couldn't get the parts out of Ford's Parts Depot, and would need to go to an independent parts store or another Ford dealership to fix a customer's vehicle. But, when Cappy questioned them, neither could come up with receipts for the "alleged" purchases. Totally busted.

Cappy wasn't through. Just who was the Ford Service representative signing off on the warranty claims that, again, were 100 times greater than the average dealer? His name – at least his initials – E.C. Cappy then matched up E.C.'s (the rep's) travel itinerary and the "E.C." (Ahem, extra cash) warranty claims. Cappy passed this information over to the New York District Sales Manager, who engaged an ex-FBI expert in lie detector equipment. The two of them met with the service rep who denied anything untoward. "Well, these numbers don't lie, so we need you to take a lie detector test," said the District Sales Manager. The service rep squirmed for a few seconds before looking down and saying, "Forget it. I won't pass it."

The story quaked throughout the entire system and a star was born. It was Joe Cappy.

Chapter 4
Getting on the Wrong Side of a Future Ford CEO

Cappy was on a blistering fast track, but, in his mind, on the wrong side of the track he envisioned for his career. "I was a catcher, not a pitcher. I was catching the 'bad guys' and the bad practices, but I wanted to be pitching new products and best practices," he would later say.

In the spring of 1966, he got his chance when he was one of the original team members of Norman Krandall's Market Strategy staff. The staff was made up of nine of Ford's up-and-coming executives, reporting to a brilliant manager, Jack Maroni.

The team, according to Cappy, "were like business consultants milking the best ideas globally from Ford's Worldwide Operations. And, we all had fire in our bellies."

Led by Krandall and Maroni, the team scoured the globe and quickly put out a "Worldwide Market Strategy Study" to share Ford's best ideas, whether they came from Germany, England, Mexico, or the United States. One of the exceptional young executives Cappy met at Ford of Britain was Alex Trotman, a young Scot who would later become Ford's CEO. "One smart guy," Cappy would recall.

When their VP, Paul Lorenz, shared this strategy book with Chairman Henry Ford II, "The Deuce" as he was known, Ford called the recommendations "a breath of fresh

15

air." When you are a Young Turk on a team that the founder's grandson positively calls out, it is the definition of a good thing.

From there, Cappy brought the "milking theme" to his next job as he kept moving up the ladder in marketing and market planning stints, first in the company's money machine – Ford trucks – led by future Ford Chairman Phillip Caldwell. It was also his introduction to nasty corporate politics, nowhere more than in the boy's club of the U.S. auto industry, completely dominated by two players – General Motors and Ford Motor Company. (The Japanese were just bit players in the U.S. market, as in the mid-to-late 1960s, "Made in Japan" meant crap.)

Next, as part of the Ford Division marketing plans team for Ford light trucks (the pickup trucks and vans), Cappy got together with product planners, engineers, marketing, advertising and sales folks who helped develop a plan to bring the best product ideas to Ford's cash cow. The plan, a book labeled Light Truck Market Strategy, was sent to Caldwell and Lee Iacocca, the President of Ford Motor Company, by Ford Division VP and General Manager John Naughton. Caldwell offered a left-handed compliment to Cappy, the still-young team leader: "Nice job done. But." There always seems to be a big "but" in corporate politics. Caldwell continued: "Not the way we should be operating!" Cappy then responded to the Ford corporate bigwig: "It was a team that came up with this

16

effort Mr. Caldwell, including your product planners and light truck engineers." Cappy ended his correspondence: "Mr. Caldwell, it won't happen again."

But, it would.

As Ford's top "boys" were fighting for command of the company, Phil Caldwell was in open battle with one of the most brilliant executives in the history of Henry Ford's company: Hal Sperlich. Sperlich would, within a decade, be trying to convince Ford to get into a new segment he was trumpeting: a front-wheel-drive van that anyone could drive, perfectly-suited for families. His idea: the minivan. But almost a decade before that, large, commercial vans were the going faction, like Ford's Econoline van and the Chevrolet G20 Cargo Van. As America was saying goodbye to the 1960s, the folks at General Motors were trying to modernize vans, and they came up with the idea of a sliding side door instead of fully-opening side doors. Ford spooks had heard what was happening at their biggest rival and Cappy got adamant about it. "These vans operate in tight places, like the city streets of New York. We've gotta have the same feature."

But Phil Caldwell wasn't convinced. He agreed it was a "nice feature," but what would it cost? Caldwell wanted research on a product feature that did not exist. Cappy was incredulous. It seemed like a no-brainer to Cappy and Caldwell's reticence was mind-blogging.

Soon enough, Caldwell was promoted to the head of Philco, Ford's electronic division. He needed one or two more stops to get nearer to the top should there need to be a replacement for Lee Iacocca, the raspy president now starting to bump heads with "The Deuce," Chairman Henry Ford II. Caldwell's replacement as head of Ford's trucks? Hal Sperlich. Cappy saw the opening and asked for breakfast with Sperlich at 6:30 a.m. the next morning at The Glass House, Ford's HQ in Dearborn. Cappy had one agenda item: the sliding door on a commercial van that General Motors had just introduced in the marketplace while Ford, thanks to Caldwell, was punting on. Cappy gave Sperlich the paper written by his team, the one Caldwell sanctimoniously had shoved up his ass. Sperlich okayed the project in 15 minutes. But, Caldwell was not done. While at a separate division of Ford, he heard about the approval of the sliding door project and told the Ford Light Truck Planning chief Jim Englehardt to track and find market research to prove the "Cappy" sliding door feature was a waste of money and prove Cappy wrong. The tracking and research continued even after Ford had the sliding door in the marketplace. Sperlich green-lighted the program and within months after introduction of the feature on Ford Econoline vans, the company was eating Chevrolet's lunch...again.

Whatever damage to Cappy, despite his success to win over Sperlich, he was reassigned to a new position. Ed

Williams, on his way to a VP job, together with an up-and-coming Ford marketing guy, the ginormously large Joe Campana, had convinced Ford management to enter recreational vehicles or the "RV" market. Gas was still relatively cheap, despite the looming oil price cartel and a crisis in America, and Ford thought they could do it better than Winnebago and the other RV companies. For Cappy, it was both good and bad news. It was a stupid assignment in what proved to be a failed venture, but it meant something all auto execs dreamed of: an executive roll position that shared in executive compensation – annual bonuses that often dwarfed annual income. It was hitting the motherlode in the great years and made your wife forgive you for the 12- to-14 hour work days, with country club memberships, a second home, clothes and jewelry, plus great restaurants and foreign travel.

Cappy recalled: "RV product planner Roger Maugh was handed the same pile of crap, but he was stuck with building the first product already underway. It was a Fiberglas slide-in camper for the Ford F-150 pickup. It was to be made in Indiana by workers "without" a mouthful of tacks, since it was Fiberglas and would be formed in one gigantic mold. The worst was yet to come, however, because it was made of Fiberglas material that no matter how long it aged, it smelled – bad. But it looked great from a distance!

Cappy was charged with franchising Ford RV dealers and put together a small, but solid Ford truck dealer RV network. The dogs, however, wouldn't eat the dog food. And existing sellers of RVs were not buying what Joe was selling. "Use our stuff, Ford, we don't need your shit."

Cappy moved on quicker than an Airstream on 1-80 in Colorado. Cappy, trying to improve his career, went into the "field" to work for Ford sales in the Detroit district and later in the Louisville district. It was like a revolutionary leader leaving the country after a failed coup, only to be brought back to win the day again after the regime that kicks him out fails. Cappy was brought back to Dearborn as an assistant to the popular and well-liked Gordon Mackenzie, who he had worked for earlier at Ford Division. In a cost-cutting effort, as the auto industry was shrinking, Mackenzie went from Group VP to Lincoln-Mercury Division VP and General Manager. Mackenzie brought Bob Rewey and Joe Cappy with him as his two top aides as General Sales Manager and General Marketing Manager respectively.

Cappy's brightest and most challenging days were in the not too distant future, at America's smallest auto company, where he would go from a very senior position to the top of the heap – as his new company went from disaster to near-greatness, to the biggest takeover in automotive history at the time. Not bad for The Mayor of Wisconsin Dells.

Chapter 5
The Real Beginning: Clash of the Titans

Okay, to go into the detail of how American Motors became American Motors would bog down this book and miss the point of this inevitable, incredible story. In a sentence: the company started at the beginning of the 20th Century, as most automakers did: originally as bicycle makers, merged and remerged with other upstart companies through the 1920s, 30's and 40's, consolidated and became AMC in 1954, and bought Jeep in 1970. Voila! There, done.

But that would be unfair to the men and women who built what eventually became AMC from the ground up with blood, sweat, tears and some of the most interesting personalities in automobile history.

The man that got it all started was Charles W. Nash. Nash was "Henry Ford" without a portfolio. Yet, he was one of the most successful and influential men in the early automotive industry. Charles Nash went from poverty to great success in business; from a ward of the court and an indentured servant at age seven, to President of General Motors and then Nash Motors; a true rags-to-riches story.

Historically, Charles Nash stands as a peer with the other great legends in automotive history. He wasn't a development engineer, or innovative automotive developer, or plant layout expert like Henry Ford, the Dodge Brothers, or Walter P. Chrysler. But he was an astute, conservative, and successful general manager in the production and assembly of automotive products. He was a role model for managing automotive plants, equipment, and people in a fiscally conservative manner. Nash was also personally intertwined with personalities of his time, and their progeny that continued, amazingly, to be part of the heritage and future of his final endeavor, Nash Motors.

A self-taught young boy, Nash toiled as a farm worker, sheep owner, hay presser, farm foreman, farm manager, store clerk, factory worker, factory foreman, department superintendent, factory superintendent, general superintendent of an entire operation for carriages, and a farm owner.

In the carriage business (for those too young, carriages were propelled by horses – the original "horsepower" in this country), his path crossed that of the legendary William Crapo (Billy) Durant, who had started the Durant-Dort Carriage Company that evolved into the Buick Motor Company. Nash had gone to work for Durant at the carriage company. Nash's work ethic and success resulted in Durant continuing to promote Nash to higher positions of responsibility.

Billy Durant continued to expand his horizon, establishing the now behemoth General Motors on September 16, 1908, with his original Buick Company, and then bought Olds Motors and Cadillac Motor Company, followed by Oakland Motor Car (later known as Pontiac). This rapid expansion on borrowed capital with only moderate results required the infusion from the Bank Syndicate, which financed Durant's acquisitions in order to protect the bank's investment in August 1910 and keep Billy Durant and General Motors afloat.

The lead banker for the bank syndicate was James Storrow, a Boston investment banker from the firm of Lee, Higgins & Company. Storrow became actively involved in the affairs of General Motors and quickly clashed with Durant, but then famously made Charles Nash his protégé.

On September 9, 1910, Nash was appointed President and General Manager of Buick Motors. He was 46 years old.

Since fabricating and assembling mostly metal automobiles was quite different from wooden carriages, Storrow saw the need for an experienced manager to help Nash run the enormous Buick plant in Flint. And Storrow knew just the man. As a Director of American Locomotive Company (ALCO), Storrow knew Walter P. Chrysler – yes, that Chrysler – who had brilliantly managed ALCO's Pittsburgh Locomotion Erection Shop. (OK, stop the snickering.)

In spring of 1911, Storrow and Nash met Walter Chrysler in Pittsburgh and made him an offer to join Buick. Chrysler took the job at a 50 percent pay cut because he wanted to work in the aspiring automotive manufacturing business – the "new" people mover as the 20th Century evolved.

Walter Chrysler arrived in Flint, Michigan, in January 1912 and quickly revolutionized the manufacturing methods used at Buick, cutting costs and increasing production. He helped lead the company from producing just under 20,000 vehicles in 1912 to about 125,000 four short years later. Rock on!

But the new General Motors' financial condition continued to drift despite the production increase, resulting in the Bank Syndicate ousting founder Billy Durant, and replacing him briefly with James Storrow and then Thomas Neal. Charles Nash became a VP of General Motors in July 1912, and on November 19, 1912, was appointed President of General Motors. And, importantly, Walter Chrysler assumed the role of President and General Manager of the biggest part of General Motors, Buick.

The team of Storrow, Nash and Chrysler dramatically improved the performance of Buick, and therefore, General Motors.

Meanwhile, original founder Billy Durant was undeterred and was busy attempting to find a way to wrest control of "his GM" away from the Bank Syndicate. He formed a new company, Chevrolet Motor Company, in November 1911, to compete with Henry Ford's new and grossly successful and groundbreaking Model T. Over the next four years, using money earned at Chevrolet and other sources, Durant bought GM stock at every opportunity. Durant pulled out all the stops, securing the assistance of Pierre Du Pont – yes, the chemical magnate – who purchased a large block of GM stock, thereby allowing Durant to gain back control of General Motors.

Back in charge, Billy Durant restructured the Board of Directors and made Pierre Du Pont the company's Chairman of the Board. Charles Nash made the mistake of supporting James Storrow's efforts to reinstitute a voting trust for GM and reverse Durant's victory. The relationship between Nash and Durant was toast. Durant considered Nash a traitor and a liar. Charles Nash was finished at General Motors.

But, Billy Durant knew that he couldn't lose Charles Nash and Walter Chrysler at the same time, so he made Chrysler an offer he couldn't refuse – a ten-fold increase in salary, loads of stock in the company and a seat on General Motors' Board.

However, without Nash as a buffer, Walter Chrysler fought with Billy Durant constantly and stayed at GM for just three years, leaving in October 1919.

Walter Chrysler greatly admired Charles Nash as an automotive executive. "Charley Nash was precisely the man needed to guide General Motors through the condition in which he found it when he left the Durant-Dort Carriage Company in Flint to become the president of Buick. Nash may have known little about automobiles when he began in

1910, but he did know how to handle men; he knew how to run a factory. Above all, he was loyal; you could not find a man more honest."[1]

Chapter 6
On With a New Show!

Being unsuccessful in regaining control of General Motors, James Storrow attempted to buy Packard Motor Car Company and was prepared to appoint Charles Nash as President and Walter Chrysler as General Manager. Merger negotiations with Packard shareholders, however, broke down. Also, Storrow and Nash were unable to convince Walter Chrysler to come along for the ride. While this breakup ended the longstanding teamwork of the three men, they all remained good friends.

Storrow and Nash then proceeded to acquire the Thomas B. Jeffery Company, which like so many of the early car companies got into the business after first making bicycles. Nash was installed as President. According to Nash, "They chose Jeffery because they believed it had been founded and conducted along sound business lines. Charles Jeffery, son of the founder, likely sold the business due to Nash's reputation and talents...Jeffery agreed to stay on the Board and provide continuity." [2]

As expected, Charles Nash at age 52 thoroughly transformed the firm. So much so, the company name was changed to Nash Motors on July 29, 1916, shortly after its purchase by Storrow and Nash. Total production in 1916 was 6,725 units, less than one percent of Ford's Model T production, but under Nash's leadership, Nash Motors produced 138,169 units in 1928. Unfortunately Nash's business partner, James Storrow, Chairman of Nash Motors, did not get to witness the transformation as he had passed away two years earlier on March 13, 1926.

Under Charles Nash's leadership, Nash Motors consistently earned profits from 1917 until 1933, when they suffered a loss of $1.2 million, due to the on-going impact of the Great Depression. The Company suffered modest losses for the next two years, but rebounded with a small profit in 1936.

"Nash brought many changes into Nash Motors that lowered costs and improved productivity. He instituted "straight line production," where the complete production process moved ahead progressively from one end of the factory to the opposite end. This closely resembled Henry Ford's Highland Park plant, and was what Walter P. Chrysler installed at Buick."[3]

Nash also cleared the plant of all the old machinery, and, for its time, brought in "high tech" manufacturing capabilities, sometimes at great expense. Most important, the trucks Nash Motors built were in demand, especially the four-wheel-drive versions the U.S. Army craved during World War I. As the company succeeded it got bigger, buying the control (and later all) of the Seaman Company in 1919 to create "closed car body" passenger cars.

"By 1925, Nash employed 13,000 workers, purchased materials from hundreds of Wisconsin-based suppliers, and had 150 dealers within the Wisconsin borders. Nash Motors was Wisconsin's largest taxpayer ($880,000). At that time, Nash Motors' value to the State exceeded the total production value of Wisconsin's dairy industry."[4]

"An investment of $100 in Nash Motors' stock in 1916 was worth $4,750 by December 1927. The Company's peak daily production, from their three (Wisconsin) plants in Kenosha, Racine, and Milwaukee, was reached on August 23, 1928, at 1,020 vehicles."[5]

While Charles Nash's leadership produced outstanding results, his business policies and practices were timeless and role models for the automotive industry. Unfortunately, all of the U.S. manufacturers have failed numerous times up to the present day, to follow Nash's common sense, practical, and successful policies. In a nutshell, Nash believed in putting the dealers ahead of the manufacturer and making sure they were profitable selling and servicing vehicles for the buying public. After all, they were the manufacturers' real customers, not the men and women buying the vehicles

Sadly, much of Nash's philosophy has been often ignored in every generation of leadership in the automotive industry – somewhat like a bad cancer cell that you can't entirely eliminate and keeps returning.

By 1934, Charles Nash was 70 years old and tiring, was increasingly disconnected from his company, and was looking for complete withdrawal from the business. However, he needed to find a worthy successor.

Surprisingly, it was Walter Chrysler that provided Charles Nash with the "perfect" candidate to succeed him, a man by the name of George W. Mason. Mason was President of the Kelvinator Corporation, a leading manufacturer of household refrigerators and commercial refrigeration equipment. Refrigerators to autos? Actually Mason was no stranger to the auto industry. He had joined Kelvinator after learning mechanical engineering and business administration at the University of Michigan, working for Studebaker and then Dodge, and then in 1921, becoming the head of manufacturing of automaker Maxwell-Chalmers at the ripe old age of 30.

But to lure Mason to Nash Motors, Charles Nash had to buy Kelvinator – a merger that was completed in October 1936 and approved by the stockholders in late December, and yet a new company name, Nash-Kelvinator.

Chapter 7
By George: Mason and Romney, American Motors is Born

Charles Nash found in George Mason the perfect individual to carry-on with "his" company in the same manner and approach that Nash espoused—he was a kindred spirit. Mason had successfully run Nash-Kelvinator Motors from the end of the Depression Era into the World War II period. As happened with all U.S. auto manufacturers, Nash-Kelvinator went to war becoming what would be known as "The Arsenal of Democracy." The last pre-war Nash car was built in January 1942.

The Nash plants in Wisconsin were converted into the production of bomb fuses, rocket motors, Pratt-Whitney aircraft engines, helicopters, propellers, carburetor castings, and binoculars, until 1945 when the plants were reconverted into automotive production.

"From a pre-war production peak of 89,000 vehicles, the post-war economic boom brought production up to 250,000 vehicles."[6] It was a seller's market, resulting from the pent-up demand and return of our soldiers. The auto manufacturers could sell all that they could build – the same boom took place with household appliances and Kelvinator was also selling everything they could build, more than doubling their pre-war production.

Some savvy business leaders of the time, however, knew the euphoria of a seller's market would not last. Plus, the Big Three automakers, General Motors, Ford and Chrysler, had the capital to invest heavily in new product and produce vehicles in higher volume at advantageous prices. George Mason knew he had to read the tea leaves properly. He knew that he couldn't compete successfully in the expected broader and larger marketplace. He needed to find some other independent automakers to merge with for future growth and prosperity, by sharing chassis, components, and plant facilities.

In looking around the smaller auto manufacturers, his eye landed on Packard Motor Company and Hudson Motor Company. In fact, Packard Motors and Nash-Kelvinator had engaged in early discussions in both 1946 and 1948 without any results.

Enter George Romney. In 1948, the same year Nash founder Charles Nash died, Romney joined Nash-Kelvinator as Mason's assistant following a successful career as managing director of the Automobile Council for War Production and the Automobile Manufacturers Association. (He would later serve as the 43rd Governor of Michigan and a Presidential hopeful in 1968.) As Mason's second-in-command and a vice president of Nash-Kelvinator, Romney wrote a report stating, "If future merger on any scale is going to be necessary, merging NOW while companies are financially strong would be the soundest course."[7]

As the mating game began in earnest, Nash-Kelvinator was not taking its eyes off of product innovation and in March 1950, introduced the first modern compact car for the U.S. market. First as a convertible and later as a station wagon and hardtop sedan, the car was given a nostalgic name – Rambler – the car line made between 1908 and 1914 by the Thomas B. Jeffrey Company. What goes around had come around.

The mating game needs willing partners. Packard Motors, which would have been the perfect complement for Nash-Kelvinator, backed away under its president James J. Nance. Nance, at first, appeared to be a willing participant, but things just didn't work out. Mason decided to move forward and ended up merging on May 1, 1954, with Hudson Motor Company, the smaller automaker named for the founder of Detroit's famous department store, J.L. Hudson. Hudson wasn't the best partner available, but a merger, even with a weak partner, appeared to be better than none.

The merged new company also received a new name, **American Motors Corporation** or AMC. At the time, the merger was the largest-ever within the automotive industry. George Mason became Chairman, President and CEO of the new company, and George Romney was named Executive Vice President. Former Hudson president, A.E. Barit, became a director of the new Company.

An added bonus for Mason was Roy Chapin, Jr., a son of one of Hudson's founders, who joined the American Motors Board and subsequently, took a management position in the new company in November 1954 when George Romney named him Assistant Treasurer, then Treasurer; and finally, at the end of 1956, Executive Vice President and General Manager of the Automotive Division.

Chapin's father, Roy D. Chapin, had gained notoriety in the automotive world in 1901 when, while working for the Olds Motor Works in Detroit (later Oldsmobile), he successfully drove a one-cylinder Oldsmobile from Detroit to New York City – a feat never before attempted. Chapin's heroics produced widespread publicity for Oldsmobile and helped rescue the company from bankruptcy.

George Mason never got the opportunity to see how successful the merger would turn out, since within five months of the merger, he fell ill, and died in October 1954. His assistant and protégé, George Romney assumed his duties.

Romney had his work cut out for him for the next several years as the new company lost money while working to rationalize their product line-up, plants, equipment, finances, and people. American Motors continued to lose money through 1957, when George Romney decided to put all of his chips on the seven-year-old Rambler car line in a "do or die" effort and let the Nash and Hudson nameplates disappear from the marketplace.

Romney's thinking was radical at the time, since the Big Three manufacturers built only full-size cars for the marketplace. The Rambler was really an intermediate size car, although it was referred to as a compact car when introduced.

Romney knew that he couldn't compete head-on with Ford, GM and Chrysler with his full-sized Nash and Hudson cars. He didn't have the resources to compete over a broader product lineup. He needed to concentrate his capital in just one segment. The market segment where he could make inroads and profits was where he had no competition from the Big Three.

American Motors could sell an array of vehicles smaller than full-size cars to appeal to families at lower prices than the full-size car price points. In addition, the smaller cars would provide better gas mileage for lower operating costs for the consumer. This shift in strategy, along with new styling and features on the Rambler, proved successful. At the time, all of the cost cutting, consolidation, trimming of models, plant closings, layoffs and a more confident dealer body finally kicked in to boost both production and profits in 1958.

From 1958 through 1962, American Motors, having reduced their breakeven point, was profitable, even though in 1959 competition in the small car segment increased significantly.

During his eight-year-plus leadership span, Romney brought the new company to profitable levels the last six consecutive years. The Romney "small car" strategy was working like a charm.

However, the competition started to heat up as the Chevy Corvair, Ford Falcon, and Plymouth Valiant were introduced as 1959 models. Then in 1961, the Chevy II and Dodge Dart were introduced. The Volkswagen Beetle was also a high-volume seller and then in 1963, Ford introduced the 1964 model Mustang, a runaway success.

Unfortunately for AMC, George Romney was thinking about politics and running for Governor of Michigan. Romney asked the AMC Board for an unpaid leave of absence while he investigated the possibility. The Board agreed with Romney's request, and he ran and won the gubernatorial battle in 1963.

The likely candidate to replace Romney was Roy Abernethy, a solid old school salesman. Romney had hired Abernethy based upon George Mason's earlier recommendation. At the time, Abernethy, Vice President of Sales, with Romney's move to the Governor's mansion, was named president and CEO in 1963. A board member, Richard Cross, was named Chairman, presumably to act as a bookmark in the event Romney returned.

Despite AMC's previous success, Abernethy inexplicably discarded the Romney "small car" strategy. Financial disaster would soon strike.

Chapter 8
Folding With a Winning Hand

Roy Abernethy had an automotive bug all his life, starting as an apprentice auto mechanic while going to night school at Carnegie Institute of Technology. Abernethy graduated with degrees in civil engineering and automotive engineering. He then took a sales position at Packard Motor Company and rose quickly through the ranks to assistant general sales manager in 1951. In 1953, Abernethy left to join Willys Motors as Vice President and General Manager. Willys was the creator of Jeep vehicles, first for World War II and later for domestic purposes.

In October 1954, based upon the recommendation of George Mason, George Romney hired Abernethy as Vice President of Sales. Abernethy was elevated further in December 1955, when he was named Vice President for the Automotive Distribution and Marketing. In 1962, Abernethy replaced the departing future Governor of Michigan, George Romney as President and CEO.

Within the next four years Abernethy inexplicably and completely discarded the Romney-focused strategy on the small car market AMC had created in the United States, and attempted to compete across the marketplace with a broad market line-up, especially with larger, more luxurious cars. Under Abernethy's leadership, American Motors market share and profitability dropped like a stone.

It may have been his competitive spirit to challenge the Big Three, but it brought the company to its knees – facing likely bankruptcy with losses in 1966 of $12.6 million and a staggering loss of $75.8 million in 1967.

The lesson Abernethy had betrayed was never play poker with high rollers, unless you have as much or more money than they have. On top of that, Abernethy had been dealt a "pat" hand by Romney, yet, he folded.

During the debacle of 1966 and 1967, the AMC Board quickly concluded that a change at the top was mandatory. As a result, both Board Chairman Richard Cross and CEO Roy Abernethy resigned their positions – Cross in June 1966, and Abernethy in January 1967. Roy Chapin, Jr. became AMC's Chairman and CEO, while Bill Luneburg was named President and COO.

Chapin quickly dismissed Abernethy's strategy and retreated to the Romney approach of not trying to be all things to all people – and to concentrate in the areas of AMC's expertise, where they produced small cars with excellent value that people wanted to buy.

From a financial standpoint, Chapin did extremely well and over 11 years as CEO, the company only lost money in three years. But his best decision, and one that would keep the company solvent long term, was his strong desire and decision to broaden his car-only product lineup by buying Jeep from the former Willys Jeep, now known as Kaiser-Jeep. At that time in 1969, neither insiders nor outsiders saw Chapin's proposed purchase of Jeep as a good strategic move.

Chapin requested his vice president of Product Development and Manufacturing, Gerry Meyers, to inspect the Kaiser-Jeep facilities and analyze the value of the Jeep product lineup and report to the board his opinion on purchasing the company.

Meyers did a thorough examination of Kaiser-Jeep's entire operations, visited their facilities, and reviewed their product plans. His conclusion, *"don't buy Jeep."* Meyers reported his conclusion to the AMC Board and the board agreed.

Roy Chapin had a much broader view of Jeep potential than Meyers, due to his international business exposure, and was aware of the value of adding a viable truck product to his lineup. Plus, he knew of Kaiser's willingness to sell the Jeep business. Chapin had a duck hunting cabin in Canada across the Detroit River, and one of his hunting friends was Stephen Girard, Jeep's CEO.

So, in late 1969, Chapin again called Gerry Meyers in and said, "How would you like to become a group vice president?" Meyers said, "Absolutely." Chapin then told him to buy Jeep and fix all of the problems Meyers had observed and he would get the promotion. Instantly, Meyers, with his incentive in-tow, became the champion of Jeep at American Motors, and the purchase of Jeep was completed in February 1970, at a cost of roughly $70 million – a king's ransom at the time – about $500 million in today's money. It would turn out to be the bargain of the automotive century.

Chapter 9
Enter the French

Gerald "Gerry" Meyers was appointed President and COO of AMC in May 1977, reporting to R. William McNealy, AMC's Vice Chairman, and the two men instantly became rivals for the top job at the automaker.

McNealy and Meyers were requested to each prepare strategy papers on the direction American Motors should adopt going forward. McNealy's proposal suggested downsizing the company and concentrating its minimal resources on the Jeep products. Meyers' plan was to downsize, but continue as a car and truck company, with the partnership of a foreign car manufacturer providing the investment and engineering for the car products, coupled with some imported cars. AMC would then concentrate all of its resources on Jeep vehicles.

Meyers' strategy won over the Board. He got the top job in October 1978 and McNealy resigned immediately. Meyers than proceeded to recruit W. Paul Tippett as president. Tippett was executive VP and a director at Singer Company. Tippett also had automotive experience at Ford Motor Company, as a former president of STP Corporation, which produced engine oils, etc., as well as five years of marketing experience with Proctor & Gamble.

Meyers soon began pursuing an alliance with another manufacturer and had his eye in the direction of France, where passenger cars ruled the market, trucks existed only for commercial use, and Jeep-like vehicles were a freak-of-nature. It turned out that one French manufacturer, Peugeot, was seriously interested in pursuing the idea with American Motors. Actually, it was believed to be a "done deal."

Gerald Meyers went so far as to schedule a press conference in Chicago to provide information on the merger between AMC and Peugeot. Pete Guptill, a rising sales manager, was assigned to pick up Meyers at O'Hare International Airport and drive him to the conference venue on the top floor of the Standard Oil Building in downtown Chicago. It was Chicago Auto Show time and interests in all things automotive in the Windy City were uppermost in the mind of the media. It was the perfect time to make a groundbreaking announcement that would "rock" the automotive world. The conference room was ready for Meyers and the press, lavishly adorned with top-shelf food and drinks. Cocktails of shrimp were big enough one could put a saddle on them and ride them down Lakeshore Drive. No expense was spared.

Guptill picked up Meyers on the curb outside of baggage claim, Meyers got in the front passenger seat and then turned to Guptill and said, "Well, Pete, what's up?" Guptill thought it was just small talk, but answered that everyone on his sales team was excited about the press conference and the news about the deal with Peugeot.

"Well they're going to be disappointed, because there is no news and no deal, as of now," Meyers said matter-of-factly. Guptill was stunned as was everyone in attendance at the "press conference." It was a complete bust – the biggest "nothing burger" in the history of nothing burgers. The American Motors team in attendance were looking at each other with a collective thought: "What just happened here? Are we back to where we started or, rather, how will this end?"

After the Chicago debacle, AMC's team went back to work on the usual grind of keeping the company afloat in the market. But soon, another rumor about a possible suitor arose. Meyers had found a willing foreign partner, Renault, the state-owned French automotive company, which in 1977 was the world's sixth largest vehicle maker selling 1.1 million cars and 175,000 trucks. Of this worldwide total, Renault sold only 13,200 Renault cars – the quirky little Le Car – in the U.S. marketplace.

American Motors and Renault signed a proposed arrangement in March 1978, where AMC would first distribute and eventually manufacture Renault cars in North America.

By January 1979, the agreement stated that Renault would sell Jeep vehicles in Europe and South America. It would also create a partnership to develop a new line of Renault passenger cars to be built in North America. Both Meyers and Renault president Bernard Hanon said the agreement involved no exchange of money, no purchase of AMC stock, and no plans for Renault to sell AMC passenger cars.

Within nine months, reality set in when AMC's Balance Sheet and profit forecasts were reviewed. In October 1979, Renault announced plans to invest directly in American Motors. Renault would buy 1.5 million shares of AMC stock (5 percent of the total) for $15 million, and provide an additional $135 million in loans. If the loans were converted into shares, Renault would own 22.5 percent of AMC's stock. Renault would also make available to AMC about $50 million in working capital. In return, Renault Chairman and CEO, Bernard Vernie-Palliez, immediately took a seat on the AMC Board.

And then the wheels started coming off the wagon. AMC would record losses in 1980 and 1981 of $200.8 million and $136.6 million, respectively. In late September 1980, AMC sent to its shareholders a proposal asking them to approve a plan for Renault to acquire as much as 59 percent of the company. Shareholders overwhelmingly approved the plan on December 16, 1980. Renault purchased an additional $200 million in AMC stock, giving it a 46 percent ownership share. In mid-December 1980, a group of American and French banks gave AMC a five-year unsecured credit line of $250 million.

Renault added four more directors to the AMC Board: Paul Percie du Sert, Renault's Deputy VP of Finance;

Pierre Semerena, Renault's Director of International Business; Rudolph Lambert, Renault's Director of North American Operations; and Felix G. Rohatyn, a Lazard investment banker in New York City. Lazard was, and is, an investment firm originating in the mid-1800s, and some believe Rohatyn "invented" the merger and acquisition furor of the late twentieth century. At this time, December 1980, there was absolutely no question as to who was in control of American Motors – there was also no question that American Motors would be in bankruptcy without Renault's capital infusion, credit, and support.

AMC losses continued steadily: a $153.5 million loss in 1982 and a $258.3 million loss in 1983—almost three quarters of a billion dollars in losses for the period 1980 to 1983.

Along with the financial losses was the loss of confidence in Meyers by Renault. A good amount of lost goodwill came from Meyer's relationship with the ranking Renault ex-pat at AMC, José Dedeurwaerder. José's expertise was in manufacturing and product and he was brought in to oversee the launch of the first Renault product built in the U.S. – what would later be named the Renault Alliance.

When José arrived in Southfield, Michigan, in 1981 to head-up manufacturing and product development, he asked Meyers where he should look for a home. Meyers suggested that José consider locating close to the old

Kelvinator plant where all of the product development and engineering took place. The area around that plant in Detroit was run down and surrounded by low-income housing and getting worse by the day as the City of Detroit continued on its downward trajectory. José never forgot that slight and subsequently bought a home in the same toney suburb where Meyers lived.

Meyers was constantly trying to prove to José that he was, in fact, in charge. For an early top level executive meeting, the room, as normal, had been set-up with tables forming a square, with no distinction as to the head of the room. José arrived early and took a seat. When the attendees were all in place, Meyers walked in and stood behind José, saying, "You are in my seat." José, red faced, scrambled to find another seat.

In January 1982, Gerald Meyers, after a disastrous tenure, was forced to resign, and was replaced as Chairman and CEO by Paul Tippett. José Dedeurwaerder replaced Tippett as president and COO.

Chapter 10
A Cup of Joe...Cappy

On February 19, 1982, Joe Cappy joined American Motors after 26 successful years at Ford Motor Company, where he had risen to become general marketing manager for the Lincoln Mercury Division. Joe left Ford in an attempt to get a "double bump" to officer level at AMC. It possibly could have happened at Ford, but he felt it was at least three years off. In addition, the automotive industry was still in a rut thanks to the recession that had doomed Jimmy Carter's presidency, and, perhaps worse, Ford's product cupboard was bare.

Going through the interview process at AMC in late 1981 should have provided Joe with a wake-up call. Joe was interviewed by the Chairman, Gerry Meyers, and President, Paul Tippett, and was left waiting for several months without a call back with a yes or no response. Then after the first of the year, Meyers was out as chairman and replaced by Tippett.

Finally, Cappy was contacted again for the position of Vice President of AMC's Marketing Group, including marketing, advertising and North American sales, service, and parts. He was asked if he would come back for interviews with the new team, Chairman Tippett and President José Dedeurwaerder. He said yes, and jumped into the frying pan again.

It turned out that Tippett was pleased with Joe as a candidate, but since Joe would be reporting to Dedeurwaerder, he needed to be interviewed by the Renault ex-pat. Out of the gate, Cappy was extremely impressed with José's dynamic personality and decisive manner. Cappy's only real question was the survivability of AMC. José laid out for Cappy that the company was now firmly controlled by Renault and AMC's future would be bankrolled and supported by the French Government. Joe was sold! Climb aboard!

After 26 fruitful years, Joe Cappy was leaving Henry Ford's car company. But one thing he would not leave behind was something he had been engrained with as he rose through the ranks of Ford: operate under the highest ethical standards and with consistently steadfast integrity. He did not know it at the time of his departure, but those standards and, importantly, the integrity he had learned at Ford, would challenge him and ultimately serve him and others well in just a few short years.

Joining AMC, one thing Cappy didn't realize was the rest of AMC never received José Dedeurwaerder's message about who controlled the company and where the company was headed. Cappy hit the ground running converting all of the AMC cars and future to the Renault brand, and never noticed the troops were watching him try to take the hill by himself. It was a big, early misstep. Everyone else thought it was business as usual and AMC was a pure, independent American company.

Since the new joint venture sub-compact car to be built in Kenosha, Wisconsin, was still about 18 months away, the AMC management team had decided to import a sporty two-door 2+2 vehicle called the Renault Fuego. The Fuego was an exciting car. It had attractive and distinct styling, and would have price points in the marketplace that would create significant buzz do to its relatively low price-point. Plus, it was available with a turbo-charged engine that provided the car with excellent torque and power. Its European ride and handling made it a complete driving package.

The Fuego seemed like the perfect product to pave the way for the new sub-compact built in America coming behind it. It would obliterate the stodgy old image of AMC and bring new, younger buyers into AMC dealerships. Automotive writers and designers were enamored with the car and everyone held high hopes that the car would revive AMC's fortune. Cappy told *The Wall Street Journal,* "AMC has a reputation for making cars for Joe Lunchbucket, school teachers and mailmen." Cappy believed that Renault products, beginning with the Fuego, would establish a whole new image for the company. Cappy told the press that AMC had to "catch the leading edge of the baby boomers, ages 24 to 40, to be successful." The standard Fuego would be priced at $8,500, and about $10,500 for the Turbo model, a bargain in the market.

As would often be the case, Steve Harris, Cappy's Public Relations shadow, had to follow the elephant around with a broom and clean up and correct all of the things that he shouldn't have said – since the company was still playing the independent American car company game with the public, its employees and its dealers.

As excited as Joe Cappy was for the new Renault Fuego, the AMC dealer body was even more excited, and early dealer orders poured into headquarters. In fact, based upon the early success of the car, AMC increased their production allocation from Europe by 3,500 units.

With a successful launch under its belt, attention was now being shifted to the new, small, joint-venture car, named the Renault Alliance, in both four-door and two-door models. The Alliance was a three-box car, meaning it had a trunk and was not a hatchback.

But before the first Alliance was built for public sale, disaster struck. Major electrical quality problems besieged the hugely popular Renault Fuego. The car would simply stop running while on the highway or city streets. If lucky, a Fuego driver would coast to the side of the road until a tow truck brought the dead French soldier back to the dealership. As engineers investigated, while the U.S. government safety officials climbed into AMC's shorts, the depth of the problem like a Mack Truck – it was an intermittent electrical issue that no one could predict, and, worse yet, no one inside AMC or Renault could solve. Fuego owners never knew when the problem would strike. After scores of customers became stranded multiple times, hundreds cried "lemon" and demanded the dealers refund their money. There was no Internet at this time but it did not matter: word of the defective Renault Fuego spread like wildfire. The Renault Fuego was dead on arrival.

AMC president José Dedeurwaerder couldn't understand why the sales team couldn't get the dealers to order more Fuegos arriving by ship from France. The meetings with him were very difficult. José kept extolling the virtues of the car and its wonderful styling, price, and performance. Finally, in one meeting, Pete Guptill, a new Regional Sales executive, made a point that Dedeurwaerder could finally understand. Pete said, "José, the Fuego is the most attractive-looking car sitting dead on the shoulder of all the highways in the country. Our dealers call the car, the "NO GO, FUEGO."

Ouch. But all was not lost, except Joe Cappy's respect for his boss José Dedeurwaerder.

Chapter 11
Feet of Clay

Joe Cappy had extremely high expectations for his relationship with his immediate supervisor, AMC President José Dedeurwaerder. He saw José as an exceptional executive, superior to most of those he observed first hand at Ford Motor Company. It was exciting to work this closely to a dynamic leader.

It was obvious that José had a temper that flared quickly, but Cappy could live with that since he knew what was expected of him and could deliver the results. José was a no-nonsense executive.

As was his custom, Cappy maintained long hours that began at 7:00 a.m. and continued to 7:00 p.m., with more to do after dinner. Everyone at that time was pushing hard to get the company moving again after the disastrous Roy Abernathy and Gerald Meyers "reigns of error."

Two of AMC's northeast sales managers, Harlan Haywood and Jack Polan, asked Cappy if it were possible to have Dedeurwaerder come to New York City for a dinner meeting with about a dozen large dealers selected from the region – greater New York and Washington/Baltimore. It was their belief that José could give these dealers the inspiration and motivation as to what they could expect once the new Renault products began to roll into their dealerships.

Cappy approached José with a request to make an overnight trip to New York City. His calendar was loaded, but they worked out a date where they could fly out of Detroit on American Airlines in late afternoon and return the next morning. The date was set and the regional managers sent out the invitations to their customers – the dealers.

Upon landing at LaGuardia, Joe and José grabbed a taxi and headed off to the Regency Hotel on Park Avenue. As the taxi turned onto Park Avenue, José turned to Cappy and said, "Joe, I can't have dinner with you and the dealers tonight because I have an important meeting with Percy du Sert (Renault CFO) on some critical capital issues." Cappy was dumbfounded and, at first, couldn't speak. Then, just as the taxi stopped at the hotel door, he blurted out that dealers from the mid-Atlantic Region were coming to New York just to hear him. Dedeurwaerder deadpanned, "Joe, you can handle it," and stepped out of the taxi.

By the time Cappy paid the taxi driver and entered the hotel, José was leaving the front desk with his key, said hello to the two sales managers waiting in the lobby, and got in the elevator.

Cappy proceeded to tell the sales managers that José would not make the dinner and why. The men were crestfallen. They started to explain to Cappy the difficulty they had in getting this group of dealers into New York for this special meeting. Cappy stopped them and said there was nothing he could do. After all, he had found out just as the taxi pulled up to the hotel. Cappy asked where the dinner was being held and they said just across Park Avenue at a French restaurant called Le Périgord (now relocated). They told Cappy they had specifically picked the restaurant to please Dedeurwaerder. Cappy sighed and then said he would just drop his bag in the room, freshen up and be right down.

Upon entering Le Périgord, the three men walked to the back of the room where tables had been arranged for the dealer group. All of the invited AMC dealers were present. After introductions and handshakes, Cappy, with his back to the front of the restaurant proceeded to explain why Dedeurwaerder couldn't join them – very important and "pressing" issues that had come up that he needed to attend to that evening.

Just then, one of the dealers facing the front of the restaurant said he thought he knew what needed to be "pressed." He told Cappy to turn around. Walking across the front of the restaurant was José with a young and very attractive blond woman about to be seated in a booth on the sidewall.

Cappy called out to José, who took one look, never blinked and walked back to the dealer table, said "Hi guys," and shook everyone's hand. Then, he quickly returned to his booth...and his blonde. Henry Ford II wasn't the only one to utter, "Never complain, and never explain."

While things of this sort with Ford executives likely occurred in private, in his 26 years at the company, Cappy had never observed such blatant mixing of business with "pleasure." It was a blow to his high expectations for José. His idol had feet of clay. And this would just be the start.

Chapter 12
Remain Calm

Conditions (other than the "little" Fuego disaster) couldn't have been better to introduce the new Renault Alliance as a 1983 model year car. It was a small, but roomy vehicle, offered in two- and four-door body styles, with all of the latest technology available in the industry, coupled with eye-popping fuel economy (52 miles per gallon on the highway). Its ride and handling were better than any of its small car competitors. In addition, it was going to be positioned and priced with its primary competitors—but the only one to seat five passengers comfortably. It was a home run in the making, made in the good ol' U.S.A.

The Renault Alliance was a marketer's dream. And best of all, the Renault brand was a "clean sheet of paper" in the U.S. marketplace, despite the Fuego hiccup. Cappy would later quip that Fuego, Spanish for "fire," was appropriately named as he was sure a ton of people got fired for the engineering snafu.

Cappy was confident that his marketing skills coupled with a sure-hit product were the recipe for success. He hadn't done his time in the trenches at Ford to blow it here. He was certain that if presented properly, the Alliance would be a major success. It couldn't miss, he thought, even though the Alliance would be competing in the most fiercely competitive and price-sensitive market segment of all, representing 30 percent of the entire U.S. market – and, against 23 competitors from all of the world's top manufacturers, including the aggressive Japanese automakers, who were beginning to gobble up market share.

To ensure success, Cappy intended to utilize all of the marketing and advertising creative brains at his disposal. AMC worked with two advertising agencies: Grey Advertising for its AMC cars and Compton Advertising for its Jeep vehicles. Cappy planned to play "jump ball" and have both advertising agencies compete for development of the advertising strategy and creative plan for the introduction of the new Renault Alliance. Even though Compton had been marketing Jeep vehicles, it was time to give them a shot at marketing cars, if they earned it. While this approach was ideal for AMC, the ad agencies were concerned—was AMC going to consolidate its advertising from two to just one agency?

Cappy made it clear from the start that it wasn't a contest for the business. Regardless of who won, Grey would do the actual "advertising". Despite deep concerns, both agencies quickly agreed to the dual creative approach.

Bill Giles, senior VP and creative director at Grey commented, "We were disappointed, but at the same time, we probably would have done the same thing. There is nothing like a little fire to make everyone dance faster."

John Dumars, Senior VP on Jeep at Compton said, "It was a painful experience."

Literally hundreds of marketing campaigns were taken to storyboard stage. Each agency ended up with four campaigns that were tested on focus groups. Two per agency went into the finals. Animatics (cartoon style drawings packaged like a television commercial) were prepared and more focus groups brought in. Cappy believed that he could have used anyone of the four campaigns and have an excellent launch. Ultimately, a creative campaign from Grey was chosen, called "Chasm."

Madison Avenue magazine, in an article by Michael Knepper, the former executive editor of *Car and Driver*, pointed out "the Renault Alliance marketing and advertising plan was as carefully developed as any in Detroit history."

The next step in the process was to seek out the most efficient placement for the creative. In the past, management hadn't given the ad agencies the leeway to buy airtime ahead. As a result, the ad agencies purchased a lot of ineffective, last-minute spot-buys. These spot-buys were typically available because no one wanted them. Talk about no-shit-Sherlock. Grey was told to make commitments, buy ahead, and get on prime time for as large a qualified audience as possible.

With this newfound flexibility, Grey started carefully buying airtime to best showcase the Renault Alliance.

Bruce McRitchie, Senior VP for Grey said, "We wanted an early jump on the competition—we knew we couldn't outspend them. We had to outsmart them, so we got in early when we could get some domination."

Then, AMC got lucky. The Alliance advertising started in early September with the U.S. Tennis Open. September was wide open and the Alliance's official launch was September 22nd. The big hitters, GM and Ford, were waiting for the NFL games to start. Then the NFL players went on strike and a mad scramble was on. But, competitors couldn't get the time slots and television networks AMC already had secured.

The Renault Alliance was also hard news, what we call "free media," as the first product of the AMC and Renault marriage. Steve Harris and his product PR staff laid out a 40-city tour of executives and cars that were extremely well received by all media types – newspapers, television, radio and automotive enthusiasts. In fact, it was successful beyond all expectations.

Harris, an up-and-coming PR star, who later in his career would serve as the PR chief of Chrysler and eventually General Motors, fondly reflected over these successful events – especially one where he accompanied Joe Cappy on a western U.S. media tour. Harris had secured a one-hour interview for Cappy with Michael Jackson, a radio talk-show host with a vast listening audience up-and-down the west coast.

Jackson introduced Cappy on the air and then started asking him questions about AMC, Renault, and the star attraction, the Renault Alliance. Cappy responded like a slugger hitting batting practice – every shot went over the wall. It was a magnificent performance, at least in Cappy's mind, and Harris, on the other side of a glass panel, had a smile ear-to-ear.

Michael Jackson then indicated that he had time for just one more question. He asked, "Mr. Cappy, you worked for a very large company, Ford Motor, for 26 years, and now you are working for a very small company, AMC. What is the biggest advantage of working in a small company versus a large company?"

Cappy quickly replied, "Michael, in a small company you are able to make faster decisions." Jackson started to thank Cappy and sign-off when Joe interrupted him and voluntarily added a post-script, "Of course Michael, they aren't always the best decisions." Harris later said, "With my nose to the glass, I started to slide down the glass panel like a slug." Cappy had learned a valuable lesson: when the media stops asking questions, stop providing answers.

In the end, the Renault Alliance, as is often the case, was its own best marketer. The initial sales goal for the vehicle was 100,000 units, three times the number of Renault-branded vehicles sold in the United States in 1981. AMC actually ended the 1983 model year with a total of 140,000 Alliances sold.

In the spring of 1983, the Renault Alliance won the auto industry's most coveted prize, ***Motor Trend Magazine's*** "Car of the Year Award." The Alliance won six of eight of ***Motor Trend's*** testing categories and came in second in the remaining two. Importantly, the winning attributes confirmed the product advantages being advertised: ride and handling; performance; passenger comfort; fuel economy, and value.

In its first month of full sales, the all-new Alliance was the seventh best seller in its segment of 23 models. By March, it was fourth ahead of such best-sellers as the Toyota Corolla, the Mazda GLC, and the VW Rabbit. It did slip a little in the summer of 1983, but only because AMC simply couldn't keep up with the steady demand.

Was the Renault Alliance a bigger success than Cappy expected? "I have to say we were very, very pleased. We hadn't planned on running out of cars. But we did," Cappy said. "In some respects, it was a nice problem to have."

However, nothing lasts forever; at least, when you are living on the edge. The Renault Alliance and Encore (a hatchback version of the Alliance) saw the market for small fuel efficient cars shift away to larger cars, and, worse yet, significant operational defects were being detected by the vehicles' owners. Faulty fuel pumps caused stalling, irregular parts or leaks in automatic transmissions, a balky engine-cooling system, and corrosion in manual steering cars led to loss of driver control, which resulted in the recall in February 1985 of 185,000 Alliance/Encores. Sales of new vehicles, naturally, slowed with the bad news.

American Motors had also shot itself in the foot in early 1983, by not being ethical with its most important input, the wholesaling of cars to its dealer body. The most important meeting an automotive manufacturing company conducts is the Programming Meeting – the one meeting that establishes the number and type of products to be produced in the coming months, to ensure that the assembly plant is adequately manned, and all of the parts and components necessary to build the planned schedule will be available on time.

The ideal production plan is to build the number of units your dealer body is willing to accept, finance, and retail, with an optimum 60-day supply of vehicles in dealer inventory. Each month, the Sales Organization meets with its dealers to reach an agreement on the number of vehicles the dealers would agree to buy over the next 90 days. The Renault Alliance was a new product without a history and in the midst of finding its place in its segment. So, while the company was ramping up production to meet expected consumer demand, being on the same page with the dealer body was the most critical requirement.

Likely due to a number of reasons, such as individual dealer floor plan limits, concern over selling higher volumes than AMC dealers were accustomed to, not convinced the sales rate would continue to increase, etc., the Sales Organization was not getting sufficient dealer orders to meet the established production program. Concerned about telling the AMC top brass that they couldn't get the dealers to buy their monthly quota, the field sales people attempted to hide the situation by selecting certain high volume dealers to place unsold orders with, and then, after month-end, reverse the sale of these excess un-wholesaled units. The word to describe this was, simply, deception.

In reality, the field was building an unsold order bank, a big "no-no" in the industry as it could increase every month and eventually result in a major production adjustment, plant line-speed, and a costly buildup of excess parts and components. In addition, un-sold orders are like produce in your neighborhood grocery store; after a while, if it just sits there, it rots. The Treasurer's Office discovered the problem, alerted Cappy, and he reacted quickly, firing the Vice President of U.S. Sales and replacing him with Pete Guptill.

Chapter 13
Love is in The "Air"

In September 1984, Chairman Paul Tippet relinquished his additional CEO title to Renault's José Dedeurwaerder. A little more than a year later, Tippet stepped down as Chairman. Renault replaced Tippet as Chairman with Pierre Semerena, a Renault Executive VP. Semerena would serve as AMC's non-executive Chairman, and also be the American company's first non-American Chairman.

In the beginning, AMC's new President and CEO Dedeurwaeder showed an aggressive style and a "can do" attitude that garnered support from the beleaguered American Motors troops. Maybe, just maybe, they could survive as a niche manufacturer with solid Renault products and an ever-improving and popular Jeep brand. He brought in a new manufacturing boss to clean up a flawed manufacturing process and ready the system for the arrival of a totally new product.

But times were not good. The first year of Renault Alliance sales were coming to a close amid troubling reports through the warranty system that there was an ever-increasing quality problem with the award-winning vehicle. AMC was about to introduce a sister version of the Alliance, the Encore, which was essentially a hatch back version of the Alliance. But the Encore would fail to score because, out of the gate, it was tainted with the Alliance's bad rap.

Dedeurwaerder handled the situation by becoming ever more irritable toward the AMC staff and hyper-defensive about the bad news arriving for the Renault products. Gone were the hearty back slaps and "Atta boys," replaced by accusations of failure to put a good effort behind the Renault products. Sales VP Pete Guptill went from being touted by Dedeurwaerder as a viable candidate for Renault worldwide sales manager to being accused of "not wanting to sell the Renault products."

It wasn't all bad: the Jeep brand was taking off and the profitability of the brand was off the charts. Despite that success, Dedeurwaerder ignored Jeep and kept putting the pressure on for greater Renault sales. Bad habits emerged. AMC started the downward spiral of costly rebates, subsidies, and larger advertising expenditures. The company was putting out more Renault product than the dealers could absorb, causing even more chaos in its sales channel.

Joe Cappy was well aware of the developing situation, but he dutifully continued to support Dedeurwaerder, and even promoted events that would put Dedeurwaerder in a favorable light with the AMC team. But the AMC people weren't stupid or naïve. They witnessed first-hand that the quality-plagued Renault Alliance was getting maximum support while the Jeep brand was left begging for crumbs.

Dedeurwaerder's motive became clear: as CEO of Renault-owned American Motors he needed big Renault vehicle sales in the United States to continue to import vehicle componentry from France. It was a commitment he had made to his colleagues in Paris and his ticket to an even bigger job, someday, inside the mothership.

As the product quality problems grew and the sales diminished, Dedeurwaerder's behavior became more and more erratic. He acted as a tyrannical dictator in a perpetual bad mood, rather than a leader. Joe Cappy remained an ally but it was growing thin. Cappy had the tact and diplomacy genes, and he needed every one of them to hold up Dedeurwaerder as the leader while the AMC team was growing ever more skeptical.

It didn't help that Dedeurwaerder openly engaged in a flirtation, and later more than that, with a lower-level female employee in the Kenosha, Wisconsin, operations. The abuses of the system to support the relationship completely soured his image among the AMC management team.

By then, Pete Guptill had become Group VP of Sales and Marketing. One day he was performing the ugly duty of letting go employees in what had become an annual ritual at American Motors known as the RIF (Reduction in Force). As Guptill took a break from his unpleasant task, he walked to a window and spotted the unthinkable, considering the state of the company: a few hundred feet from AMC's headquarters and in full view of everyone, Dedeurwaerder and his girlfriend were getting into a waiting helicopter to go who knows where. A private helicopter for a foreign CEO of an American company that didn't have a pot to piss in?

A few days later, after ending a two-day off-site meeting and "sleepover" at the famous Dearborn Inn that lasted until dark the second day, Guptill exited the hotel in Ford Motor Company's backyard, and made his way to the parking lot for the ride home. He and José Dedeurwaerder had identical vehicles – black Jeep Grand Wagoneers – and had parked next to each other. Under his windshield wiper, Guptill found a handwritten note thanking "someone" for "a wonderful couple of days" and promising "to see you soon."

Chapter 14
The Beginning of the End...and Hope

Lee Iacocca, Chairman and CEO of Chrysler Corporation, was one of the nation's most celebrated business executives in the 1980s, after a meteoric rise to success at Ford Motor Company in the '60s and '70s, followed by the major turn-around performance from the edge of bankruptcy for Chrysler Corporation in 1979. He had become a TV celebrity thanks to ads where he challenged Americans, "If you can find a better car, buy it." There would later be calls for Iacocca to run for President of the United States. He was too smart to be that stupid. After all, why take the pay cut?

In the mid-'80s, Iacocca was in the prime of his automotive career. He had an outstanding "feel for the market," and an exceptional cadre of senior automotive executives supporting him – probably the finest collection of automotive talent in the industry. They included Gerald Greenwald, Ben Bidwell, Bob Lutz, R. "Steve" Miller, and Hal Sperlich as his key advisors. All of his team had cut their teeth at Ford Motor Company, succeeded beyond belief, and eventually pissed off the partially family-owned "creator" of the modern auto industry. Ha, say that to the Germans at Mercedes-Benz and their heads explode.

Despite this formidable automotive team, Iacocca was concerned. The open U.S. market was drawing better and more competitive product offerings from abroad, especially the Japanese. "Made in Japan" in the 1960s meant crap. "Made in Japan" in the 1980s meant quality and value. In addition, with the exception of the highly successful Chrysler minivans the company introduced to the automotive world and changed the market for decades, their remaining other car and truck products were producing sub-par results, quality-wise and financially. Chrysler's uncompetitive, non-minivan vehicles were requiring larger and larger retail incentives to sell.

The Chrysler minivans, so hot in the market and catching all competitors flat-footed, were making most if not all of Chrysler's profits, in addition to the financing of vehicles and the sale of spare parts. CEO Iacocca and his Chrysler board decided to diversify to spread the risk. Iacocca had always been bothered by the cyclical nature of the automotive industry, which played havoc with a car manufacturer's stock price.

The answer, among Iacocca and his financial whizzes, was to form a holding company with three separate operating divisions: Car and Trucks, Financial, and Aerospace. Yes, Chrysler was building stuff for the aerospace industry. There were major internal discussions and dissentions over the strategy adopted by the board, which was to diversify with Chrysler's limited capital and people, and go forward with only the highest reward projects. While not all of the Company's executives were in agreement, the marching orders from Iacocca and the board were clear.

So, armed with sales and profit successes in 1983, just a few years after a near-brush with bankruptcy, and adoption of a new corporate strategy, Iacocca formed a Mergers and Acquisition Group. Their mission was to investigate other automotive companies, electronic companies, and other industries, such as the airplane industry, for which Iacocca had an eye for Gulfstream Airplane Company. On the latter, think about it: you are the most admired businessman on the planet, so what better way to travel than the airline industry's most desired and renowned private aircraft company.

The first M&A Team effort was within the automotive sector, with members of the team meeting with nearly every automobile company in the world from Western Europe, Eastern Europe, the Far East, and South America. The possibilities were mind-boggling, starting internationally: a major integration with German superstar BMW, which had many millions of dollars locked up in the U.S. due to heavy taxation for any dollars repatriated to Germany. The issue was what Chrysler and BMW could do to use the money in the United States to leverage it further, and what could Chrysler offer to BMW in the way of talent or components for BMW's international business.

The strategy turned domestically: Could Chrysler use idle or under-utilized American Motors plants in the United

States for the manufacturing of Chrysler products that were in demand beyond the capacity of Chrysler's plants? What about a major agreement between Chrysler and VW here in the U.S. with a sharing of products, as well as design and development for economy of scale and dealer outlets?

Other ideas included the sharing of product/engineering/marketing/ownership of automaker SEAT of Spain, which was a growing company with limited resources to grow further.

No idea was thrown away: working with Russian entrepreneurs seeking product for sale in Russia and Eastern Europe, or sharing product and distribution systems with Korean and Taiwanese car companies.

And, perhaps the most ironic possibility at the time, particularly based upon what would transpire decades later, was the Agnelli family – the owners of Fiat and its many brands – who were approaching the son of Italian immigrants, Lee Iacocca, directly, and requesting that he personally take over the automaker and run it and Chrysler together or separately. (Now, almost 30 years later, we have witnessed Fiat and Sergio Marchione take over Chrysler to work its way out of bankruptcy in a complete reversal of roles for the two companies.)

But, the biggest prize in the eyes of Chrysler management and its newly-formed M&A Team was the acquisition of the Jeep Brand from Renault.

The hunt or chase for Jeep-AMC went on for two and a half years in various forms and channels, with numerous highs and lows of interest, expectations and demands. Of interest, as well, was the open manufacturing capacity at AMC, which Chrysler's top manufacturing executive, Steve Sharf, was pointing out. At the time, with a newfound strong sales marketplace, Chrysler was capacity constrained with sales above their sustainable production capacity.

Lee Iacocca set his sights on the upside opportunity with the Jeep brand. An initial study by Chrysler's Car and Truck Division believed Jeep had too many risks and too much "baggage" and was unrewarding. Iacocca didn't agree with the study and requested the Holding Company do a similar study.

The Holding Company study showed a huge opportunity, but acknowledged a major unknown risk with Jeep CJ rollover death and injury liabilities. The CJ was the precursor to today's Jeep Wrangler. The lawsuits against the vehicles created warehouses of damaged Jeep vehicles as evidence of their defective design. But, since the Car and Truck Division turned down the Jeep opportunity to focus more on their present/future products, the Holding Company was tapped to lead the Chrysler effort to acquire Jeep – with Steve Miller and Ben Bidwell appointed team leaders to approach Renault – and, to buy AMC stock on the open market. The project was code-named "Titan."

Things started to heat up in 1986, starting with a March luncheon in a New York club between Lee Iacocca and Georges Besse, Renault's Chairman. Felix Rohatyn, a senior partner at Lazard Investment Banking and Renault's choice for a seat on the AMC Board, arranged the luncheon to introduce the two parties.

Work continued at Chrysler to explore all facets of a possible deal with Renault. In June 1986, Lee Iacocca was aboard the Qu*een Elizabeth II* with a group of Chrysler dealers on a promotional tour in Europe tied into his work on the restoration of the Statue of Liberty, a gift from France in 1886. No, the 100-year anniversary was not ironic. It is specifically why Iacocca was embracing the restoration of the lady who had welcomed his Italian mom and dad. While outside Paris, Iacocca was invited to meet again with Besse.

The two CEOs, including Iacocca confidante and top executive Ben Bidwell, met aboard a Renault-owned barge anchored on the Seine. The barge, ironically named *La Release,* was very ordinary on the outside, and appeared to be a working barge hauling freight for security reasons; but on the interior it was extremely plush and luxurious. Renault used *La Release* for private dinner parties with special guests and French government officials. At the dinner, Besse opened the subject of a buy-out of Renault's position in AMC. Both men, however, concluded such a deal was not possible at that time.

Ben Bidwell was later quoted in the news: "It's difficult to consummate a takeover on the front porch with the lights on, but we operated in the back alley with the lights off." While the project was code-named "Titan," Bidwell later said he suggested that the effort to buy impoverished AMC should have been called "Pygmy."

Pygmy, ha. It was somewhat funny considering that Chrysler had barely averted a bankruptcy in the early 80's and would later go into full bankruptcy decades later.

Meanwhile, back at the ranch, real business went on. Chrysler and AMC were already "in bed" with each having a foot on the floor and with both wearing pajamas. The companies were hammering out a contract assembly agreement whereby AMC would assemble the old and outdated Chrysler large cars and the much smaller, hardly competitive Dodge Omni and Plymouth Horizon products at the AMC plant in Kenosha, Wisconsin. Jim Donlon, VP of Finance, led the Chrysler team and Tom Foley, Executive Director Corporate Planning and Development, represented AMC. The agreement was finalized and signed in September 1986 by Gerald Greenwald, Chrysler President, and Joe Cappy, AMC President & CEO.

It was "just business," but the contract assembly talks between the two companies provided the most excellent "smoke screen" for all the other studies and discussions being undertaken by Chrysler's Titan Team that fall, and the future of one of the most important brands in the international automotive industry, Jeep.

Events heated up in early fall 1986, as Chrysler's interest increased while pressure from the French Government squeezed Renault to shed American Motors. The discussions progressed to a point of planned direct negotiations between a small team from each side.

Chrysler's team, led by Ben Bidwell and Steve Miller, was comprised of Jim Donlon, VP of Finance; Dick Goodyear, VP of Legal Staff; and Ralph Sarotte, General Manager of the M&A Automotive Group, among several others.

They were invited by Renault Chairman Besse's representatives to fly to Paris and meet with the Renault team to plan and negotiate an actual agreement in principle to complete the purchase of AMC from Renault by Chrysler. The Chrysler team was to fly first to New York City to update Chrysler's Board of Directors during their monthly meeting, and then head over to Paris to begin negotiations.

However, the night before the Chrysler board meeting, Chairman Besse's representative called to say that Besse asked for a few more days to think about the deal before negotiations could begin. The Renault Chairman was getting cold feet. It was best summed up by the Chrysler executive with the most zest for a "hook up" between Chrysler and AMC, Vice Chairman R. Steve Miller:

"Besse's last position was he wasn't going to do it. He had been there for three years investing in and pursuing a strategy of development in America. For him, it would have been a personal reversal of strategy."

Or, maybe it was because Besse had his hands full with trying to right the ship at Renault and didn't want to take his eyes off the ball. Renault, while funding and controlling AMC, was losing lots of money. That's why the French Government put Besse in place after throwing out CEO Bernard Hanon, the architect of Renault's majority purchase of American Motors.

Georges Besse was a no-nonsense leader. He discovered a disastrous situation and began challenging everything within Renault. He created an internal revolution, refocusing Renault's resources on what really mattered and commissioning several highly confidential studies to discover what sectors of the company needed to be sold, divested or completely abandoned as they had no real strategic importance for Renault.

Besse's approach was a first for Renault and completely contrary to the "normal" state-owned, socialist company spirit where the key objective was job creation with profitability an afterthought.

Despite the bleak situation he inherited, Besse had a vision and saw the benefits of Renault's alliance with American Motors, and therefore wasn't keen on giving up on it so easily, despite Chrysler's interest. After all, AMC was starting to deliver.

In the fourth quarter of 1986, AMC delivered a $20 million profit for Renault. That figure sounds like chump change today, but back then it was big; after all, since 1980, when Renault had "unofficial control" of AMC, the American company had accumulated losses over that time of $859 million. The press was stunned: the "weakling" American Motors was actually making money and its future was looking brighter by the day, thanks to Jeep. The increasing popularity of Jeep vehicles was beginning to hit on all cylinders within the most affluent classes; it had become extremely fashionable, a successful lifestyle statement of adventure, luxury, and independence. And Jeep's profit contributions were so high that they were able to offset the large losses on AMC's passenger car side.

And Georges Besse had managed to stop the hemorrhaging at Renault. Indeed, Renault started reporting a profit at the same time as Jeep started humming. A great story was unfolding. So, the question was: why break up a great team?

Chapter 15
How Not to Appoint a CEO

In October 1985, as Renault and Chrysler continued to dance, Renault and AMC executives, as well as the independent AMC directors, met in a plant outside of Brussels, Belgium, to preview the new French model destined for the shores of America. It was the new Renault 21, which would soon be imported into American Motors dealerships for sale in the United States as the Renault Medallion.

Joe Cappy, AMC's Executive Vice President of Operations, was on hand and witnessed one of the most unusual leadership episodes and CEO appointments.

Arriving on a commercial airliner from the United States were the independent AMC board members Roy Chapin, Jr., Andrew Sage, Jack Tarver, W. Paul Tippett, and Steven Girard. On the flight over, Andy Sage, fluent in French, read a French newspaper that had been aboard the plane, which was on a return leg to Brussels. The news article disclosed that Renault Chairman Georges Besse planned to promote American Motors President and CEO José Dedeurwaerder, also a Renault ex-pat, to the role of worldwide vice president of Sales and Marketing for Renault.

The independent board directors of American Motors were extremely upset over the potential loss of its president and CEO without any input, advance notice, or discussion with them. Upon landing, they requested an immediate meeting with José, who had arrived earlier to the hotel in Brussels with Jean-Marc Lepeu, AMC's CFO and Joe Cappy, the company's COO.

The sudden loss of a CEO is always traumatic, but it was even more so in this situation, even though he would be staying in the bigger global company, Renault and AMC. American Motors was in the process of building a new assembly plant in Bramalea, Ontario, Canada, as well as launching a brand new full-size passenger car built there, the Renault Premier. The planned timing for the launch of the Bramalea plant and Renault Premier was the fall of 1987.

Fact told: Renault's investment in American Motors and American Motors' future was tied to a successful plant launch and a winning product with the Renault Premier. It was a "bet the bank" situation. If it failed, AMC would fail and Renault would go back to France, its tail between its legs.

A private meeting room in the hotel was secured and the independent board directors met with Messrs. Dedeurwaerder, Cappy, and Lepeu. After confirming with José Dedeurwaerder that the newspaper account was correct, the directors inquired if José was in favor of the move, and what could they do to stop Dedeurwaerder's relocation back to Paris and Renault.

The directors brought up salary and pension benefit changes that they would be willing to consider if he elected to stay. But José indicated that he was in favor of the move, and that back in France, he would be in an even stronger position to ensure the success of both the new AMC plant in Canada and the new vehicle for the North American market.

After further discussion among the board members, along with the growing realization that José's move was possibly locked-in, the directors inquired as to who might replace him. José nodded to his left and said that COO Joe Cappy would replace him. This additional news further upset the directors, since they rightfully knew that the decision to select a CEO was the fiduciary responsibility of the American Motors' Board of Directors, and not that of the Chairman of Renault.

And then reality struck as to who was running AMC. Director Jack Tarver said, "It's not the time to lift the facade as to whom runs the Company." Andy Sage added, "We (the Board) can't do it unless José converts to a full time AMC employee."

Director Steve Girard had had enough: "Bullshit Andy. Let's get back to basics. We have a CEO and COO who have got their hands on the controls. Let José tell us what he needs from us. We should work with Mr. Besse and quit jerking ourselves off."

The meeting concluded with an indication that the directors would discuss this issue further at a dinner scheduled that night in Paris with Renault Chairman Georges Besse.

During the course of the day, including a Renault plant visit, the independent board directors gathered in small groups and had mini-discussions regarding how they planned to approach the Renault Chairman Besse that evening at dinner.

The dinner was at an elegant restaurant in the Bois de Boulogne, the Pavillion de la Grande Cascade, and a former hunting pavilion. The meal was a white glove service. Chairman Besse sat in the center of a rectangular table. Seated directly across from him was Roy Chapin, Jr., with the other independent board directors flanking his position. José Dedeurwaerder seated Joe Cappy to Besse's right, while he sat on Besse's left. Some of Renault's inside directors and other Renault executives filled in around the Besse side of the table.

After an elegant meal and dessert, Chairman Besse opened the conversation by saying that he understood that American Motors' independent board directors wished to discuss some issues with him.

Roy Chapin Jr. indicated that he was chosen as the spokesman for the American Motors independent directors, and that they were deeply concerned with Besse's decision to bring José Dedeurwaerder back to Renault while AMC was in the process of building a new plant in Canada for a new car under development for North America.

Besse indicated that he needed Dedeurwaerder's talents in a worldwide capacity that was critical for Renault's global success. He said his decision on this point was final. With Besse's position re-affirmed with finality, Roy Chapin Jr. said that under those circumstances the next subject to be dealt with was José's replacement as President and CEO. The independent directors understood that Renault's choice as the new President and CEO was Joe Cappy.

Besse made no effort to excuse Cappy from the room, and Cappy made no effort to leave – Joe Cappy had a better view than a fly on the wall, or better yet, a fly in the pudding in the middle of the table. From Besse's standpoint, having the independent board directors talking about this issue with Cappy in the room would obviously cause them considerable discomfort and likely limit their ability to speak frankly regarding Cappy's capabilities. Besse understood, and likely kept Cappy in the room for just that reason. During the entire ensuing discussion, the "Mayor of Wisconsin Dells" never said a word, nor asked a question. To speak surely would have alienated someone on the board. Cappy remained stone silent.

AMC's former Chairman and current board member, Roy Chapin Jr., went into detail regarding the AMC Board's fiduciary responsibility to select a new CEO since

AMC was a public company under U.S. laws. He concluded his remarks by saying this decision in no way reflected the board's opinion on Cappy's abilities. He said that the CEO selection process needed to be run by the AMC Board.

Renault Chairman Besse acknowledged their position, but said he believed that with a strong internal candidate that José Dedeurwaerder had confidence in, had been working closely with for more than four years, and whom the AMC Board knew as well, that a quick decision could be made.

At that point, a number of other AMC board directors offered comments, some in favor and others suggesting further review. One director, Jack Tarver, said that he would be willing to support Renault's choice of Joe Cappy, who he believed was doing an outstanding job. Steven Girard, another director, pointed out that "Without Renault's financial backing, American Motors would fail, and regardless of who the AMC Board might select, if that person and José didn't get along, the enterprise would fail." He endorsed selecting Joe Cappy and getting on with business. "We don't have time to waste," he said.

Roy Chapin Jr. and the other board directors returned to their fiduciary responsibility argument and reiterated their desire to put together a search for a CEO replacement. Renault's Georges Besse finally agreed and told Chapin to hire a search firm and begin the process. Renault would withhold their approval, however, until they reviewed the candidate that the independent directors would recommend. Besse also gave them a timetable of 90 days, after which Renault's selection of Cappy would become final.

The next day, as the AMC group was at the airport awaiting the flight back to the States, Cappy asked Roy Chapin, Jr. if he could meet with him and José Dedeurwaerder on Saturday at the AMC headquarters. It was agreed that they would meet at 10:00 am in José's office. At the meeting, Cappy explained to Mr. Chapin that he understood why the directors needed to conduct a detailed search for José's replacement and that he knew a number of top-flight executives in the industry that he respected who could be hired. Cappy said that he would have no problem working for someone of that caliber, but if the candidate they selected was not of that standard, he would look for opportunities elsewhere.

Within days, Cappy started to receive phone calls from people he knew from Ford and Chrysler, like Jim Capalongo, former Chairman of Ford of Europe, and Ben Bidwell, Chrysler Executive VP of Sales and Marketing -- both gentlemen highly regarded within the automotive industry. They all wanted to know what was going on at American Motors. Cappy gave them the straight story. Almost to a man, according to Cappy, they remarked, "I don't want to get mixed up with that mess."

In March 1986, Cappy received a call from Roy Chapin Jr. telling him the CEO job was his, as the board was disbanding the Search Committee.

An announcement was made on March 21, 1986, naming Joe Cappy, President and CEO of American Motors. For Cappy, "All is well that ends well," but the Hollywood high jinx were just getting started.

Chapter 16
A Loan or Alone

Cappy's "honeymoon" as AMC's new CEO lasted a little more than a few days when he was approached in March by his newly-minted CFO John Tierney with some troubling news: a critical capital issue that had been worked on since December 1985 had jumped to the forefront.

John Tierney had joined the company in October 1964. He was a formidable financial executive who knew AMC inside and out. His message for Cappy was that the company desperately needed to shore-up its capital to ensure that AMC could complete its new Canadian plant and introduce its critical new car due in the fall of 1987. But where would they get the money? Both Cappy and Tierney knew that its parent Renault was experiencing major financial losses in Europe, and Renault Chairman Georges Besse was laying off thousands of workers in an ugly streamlining of the company. Because of the latter, Cappy and Tierney knew it might be politically impossible to secure the additional capital from Renault for operations in North America when thousands of unionized French workers were getting pink slips.

Tierney believed that with the plans for a new world-class assembly plant and its all-new, large car – and hopefully improved bottom line performance – AMC possibly could borrow the capital needed from one or more of the big U.S. banks. Tierney believed $200 million was the minimum required to support the plan. Cappy agreed and told Tierney to proceed to explore that avenue.

It wasn't long before Tierney returned with a sobering message: not a single bank or group of banks was willing to lend AMC $200 million. To add insult to injury, Tierney also told Cappy that he had confirmed that no additional capital could be expected from Renault. Tierney believed AMC's only opportunity was to investigate the junk bond market that Michael Milken from "Drexel" had made phenomenally successful. Again, Cappy agreed: "John, let's give Drexel a try."

Drexel was an avenue open through the earlier efforts and actions by Renault's CFO, Paul Percie du Sert, who had supported Drexel in the past when a disagreement with Drexel's French affiliate Lambert developed. Drexel owed Percie du Sert and Renault a big one.

Contact was made with Drexel Burnham Lambert (the firm's full name) and, after preliminary discussions, Cappy was invited in April 1986 to Los Angeles to personally make a presentation to Michael Milken. Cappy quickly developed a thirty-minute presentation covering AMC's present situation and future plans.

Cappy and two Drexel bankers from New York City flew from Detroit to Los Angeles on a late evening plane and arrived at a hotel in Beverly Hills around 11:30 p.m. The arrangements for the next day's meeting were quite unique. Cappy had to be finished with Milken by 6:00 a.m., Pacific Time, the same time the New York Stock Exchange opened. This meant Cappy and the bankers had to arrive at Milken's Beverly Hills office at 4:00 a.m. Dressed and in the hotel lobby at 3:30 a.m., they gathered, luggage in-tow, for the short walk to Milken's office.

As the trio were leaving the hotel, a Jeep Cherokee pulled up with two people inside. This particular model was the top of the Cherokee line, adorned with gold wheels and gold trim accents. It had "bling" before "bling" was a "thing." A very attractive young lady stepped out of the passenger seat, while the driver came around to kiss and say goodbye to her. One of the bankers asked the driver, "How do you like your Jeep?" The driver shouted back, "It's me!" The bankers believed that somehow Cappy had staged the entire incident. He hadn't, but Cappy smiled, thinking of the Karma.

The trio arrived at about 3:45 a.m. at Milken's office and were guided into a conference room. At 4:00 a.m. sharp, Michael Milken walked in and wasted no time: "Tell me your story." Cappy spoke for 30 minutes. When finished, Milken weighed in and talked non-stop for the next two hours. At one point, he said, "Is $200 million enough? I can get you $500 million if you need it." Cappy was elated, thinking, "What's a few hundred millions between friends."

At exactly 6:30 a.m., Pacific Time, the phone banks in Drexel's Beverly Hills office lit up – the New York Stock Exchange was open for business on the East Coast. Milken excused himself and told Cappy and the bankers that before the group left, they should look in on his trading area.

The trio accepted his invitation and stepped into the trading area. In the middle of the bullpen was Milken with a phone to one ear, another phone in his other hand, plus an assistant with several phones in his hands to pass along to Milken when he concluded each conversation. It was a wild scene with people talking and often yelling to one another or to the assistant holding the extra phones for Milken. Seeing the madness, the visitors quietly left the mania and headed back to LAX.

Several weeks went by without any word from Drexel. Cappy and Tierney were becoming anxious, frustrated, and a bit scared. Drexel bankers repeatedly told Tierney that things were moving along. After another couple of weeks of basic silence, Cappy called New York to talk to one of the Drexel bankers himself. Cappy was told no progress as yet. With his company's future on the line, Cappy lost it: "Your hotshot Milken can't even deliver what he promised! I guess he's not as good as advertised." He slammed down the phone, steaming.

The next day, AMC CFO John Tierney came into Cappy's office and said he received a call from Drexel, and because of what Cappy said about Milken, Milken wasn't going to work on our loan anymore. Cappy called the banker himself and said, "What the hell happened?" He told Cappy, Milken got upset with what Cappy had said about him. "How did he know what I said?" Cappy asked. "I told him," the banker replied. Stupid is as stupid does. Cappy dropped everything, immediately writing a letter to Michael Milken apologizing for his comments and explaining how nervous they were about getting the loan that was essential to the company's future. He told Milken that his emotions had gotten the best of him. Cappy pleaded with Milken to continue working on raising the $200 million.

Cappy also had a battery-powered pink miniature Jeep sent to Milken's five-year-old daughter with a note thanking her father for raising money to help AMC.

Maybe it was the apology or maybe it was the pink Jeep – or both – but finally Cappy and Tierney received word that Milken would continue to work on AMC's financial needs. A short time later, Cappy received word that Milken had raised the money and AMC was provided a term sheet detailing the costs for the $200 million loan. The cost to get the funds was extremely high, but a thirsty man in the desert wasn't going to complain if the water was too warm. And AMC was certainly in a desert that was getting hotter and drier by the minute.

With the financing secured, Cappy and Tierney got on the phone to call Europe to talk with José Dedeurwaerder, who at this point was back in Renault's HQ serving as the company's head of sales and marketing worldwide, while still serving on the AMC Board of Directors; and Paul Percie du Sert, Renault's CFO, to advise them of their success. Cappy and Tierney were surprised that the Renault executives weren't as excited as they were with the success with Milken and his money. José and Paul began to talk about the high cost of borrowing and other points in the deal sheet.

Joe Cappy would have none of their babble: "Gentlemen, we need the $200 million or everything will stop dead in the water. Unless of course, Renault is willing to provide the capital we need. If not, we have no other choice." Reluctantly, the Europeans agreed. The loan closed in August of 1986.

As was discovered later, Renault really wasn't concerned about the high cost of the loan from Michael Milken and his Drexel team. Their real worry was that adding $200 million in new debt financing to the balance sheet could cause Chrysler to back off of their interest in buying American Motors. Several years later still, in talking with some Drexel executives, John Tierney mentioned the $200 million that the firm had raised for AMC. The Drexel folks remarked that the $200 million bond deal for AMC was by far the toughest junk bond sale they ever had to accomplish. It required a huge amount of arm-twisting and promises for being included, or not, in more lucrative and attractive deals to come.

For Michael Milken, his junk bond empire would soon go bust in 1989 when he was sentenced to ten years in a federal prison (later reduced to two years) for securities reporting violations after first being charged with racketeering and insider trading. The Feds fined him $600 million, three times the amount he had arranged to rescue American Motors three years prior.

Joe Cappy, Ford Motor Company's 26-year "wunderkind," joined American Motors in 1982 and here, in 1986, is the CEO. <u>The Last American</u> (Motors) <u>CEO</u>.

William Crapo "Billy" Durant started Buick Motor Co. and then merged it with Olds (mobile) and Cadillac to establish General Motors in 1908. What kind of guy has "Crapo" in his name?
(Used with permission from General Motors Corporation.)

The man who got it all started for what eventually would become American Motors. Charles W. Nash (above) was "Henry Ford" without a portfolio, yet, he was one of the most successful and influential men in the early automotive industry. He went from a ward of the court and an indentured servant at age seven, to President of General Motors and then Nash Motors.

Walter P. Chrysler arrived in Flint, Michigan, in January, 1912, and quickly revolutionized the manufacturing methods used at Buick, cutting costs and increasing production. He helped ramp up production from under 20,000 vehicles in 1912 to about 125,000 four short years later. Rock on!

Walter Chrysler provided Charles Nash with the "perfect" candidate to succeed him. George W. Mason (left) was President of the Kelvinator Corp., a manufacturer of household and commercial refrigerators. Leading Nash-Kelvinator, Mason decided to merge with Hudson Motor Co., named for the founder of Detroit's big department store, J.L. Hudson, and created American Motors Corporation or AMC in 1954. At the time, the merger was the largest-ever in the auto industry.

Mitt Romney's dad. During his eight-year-plus leadership of American Motors, before successfully running for Governor of Michigan and later a failed U.S. Presidential run, George Romney brought the new American Motors to profitable levels the last six years of his tenure. The Romney "small car" strategy worked like a charm.

The original AMC logo was graphically elegant. Not!

The American Motors' Rambler was part of CEO George Romney's strategy to only play in the "small" vehicle segment of the U.S. auto market. It worked.

Despite AMC's previous success under George Romney, newly-minted AMC CEO Roy Abernethy (right) inexplicably discarded the Romney "small car" strategy and decided to be all-things-to-all-car-buyers. Financial disaster would soon strike.

A legend's son, Roy Chapin, Jr. became legendary in his own right as his best decision, and one that would keep AMC solvent long term, was his strong desire and decision to broaden his car-only product lineup by buying Jeep from the former Willys Jeep, then known as Kaiser-Jeep. Today, his son Bill, is head of the Automotive Hall of Fame.

In January 1982, after a disastrous tenure, Gerald Meyers (left) was forced to resign, and was replaced as AMC's Chairman and CEO by W. Paul Tippett. José Dedeurwaerder replaced Tippett as president and COO.

The Renault LeCar was proof that turds are not only on the farm.

José Dedeurwaerder led American Motors under Renault's ownership. He was a brilliant automotive manufacturing executive, but had people and leadership issues due to his mercurial temper, as well as, by allowing his employees to observe his affairs while intertwining his business and "personal" life.

A true gentleman, AMC Chairman and CEO W. Paul Tippet had automotive experience at Ford Motor Company and was a former president of STP Corporation, which produced engine oils, etc., as well as five years of marketing experience with Proctor & Gamble.

Joe Cappy with Ford's Gordon MacKenzie (left) for a 25-year service pin. MacKenzie would play a huge part in Joe Cappy's career at Ford Motor Company. "He was the most enthusiastic and optimistic executive I'd ever met," said Cappy.

"No Go Fuego." It was so promising, and then, DOH, problems without answers. Doomed.

Joe Cappy and José Dedeurwaerder at the yet-to-be-completed Bramalea Plant outside of Toronto, Ontario, Canada. The image says everything about how the relationship had "developed" between the two.

Joe Cappy with the award-winning-soon-to-be-recall-plagued Renault Alliance, and baguettes. It was apropos as the car would soon be "toast." (This photo is used with permission from author and perhaps the ultimate American Motors historian Patrick Foster.)

Joe Cappy briefing former French President Valery Giscard d'Estaing (sitting, middle) about AMC's situation, just prior to the ex-President's speech to the Detroit Economic Club. Cappy is with AMC executives, including (far left) VP of Business Planning and Corporate Affairs Gerard Gastaut, (right clockwise) Board Chairman Pierre Semerena, VP of Product Engineering and Development Francois Castaing, and AMC PR Chief Jerry Sloan.

The 1984 Jeep Wagoneer (front) and Cherokee's four doors revolutionized the sport utility vehicle market by creating an entirely new segment. The Cherokee would thrive. Thirty years later, Fiat Chrysler Automobiles would revive the Cherokee name.

Chrysler CEO Lee Iacocca on a commercial
shoot. As he said, "If you can find a better car,
buy it." He was relentless in his pursuit of the
Jeep brand, for good reason: it helped him save
Chrysler from extinction. Twice.

Just after he saved Chrysler, thanks to U.S.
Government loan guarantees paid off early,
Lee Iacocca a wrote of book that rivaled the
Holy Bible in annual sales.

Nice glasses. One of the architects of Chrysler's purchase of American Motors from Renault, R. Steve Miller is the financial wiz who helped save Chrysler twice, and later saved auto supplier Delphi and Waste Management. Yes, Steve frequently found himself in the "crapper."

Ben Bidwell was an early mentor of Joe Cappy at Ford Motor Company and a genius at Chrysler. His wicked sense of humor was so dry that you needed a humidifier when you were around him.

The genius of Iacocca was recruiting the geniuses from Ford Motor Company like Gerald Greenwald (right) to reinvent a troubled Chrysler.

Later dubbed "Maximum Bob" for his product prowess, Bob Lutz, the former GM, then BMW, then Ford, then Chrysler, the back-to-GM wunderkind is a bigger legend than John DeLorean for good reason.

Lee Iacocca is considered the "Father of the Mustang", and the "Father of the Minivan", both products were game-changers that blew away the automotive industry. Hal Sperlich (right) could claim the same titles while working for Iacocca. Once Sperlich left Ford Motor Company for Chrysler, he took along his concept for the minivan product and had it under development by the time Lee Iacocca later joined him at Chrysler.

Il corpo senza vita di George Besse, presidente della Renault, assassinato da due donne di un commando di Action Directe nel novembre del 1986

Like a scene out of *The Godfather*, Renault Chairman Georges Besse's assassination in front of his daughter at the hands of terrorists temporarily killed the deal between Chrysler and the French automaker for the U.S. car company to buy American Motors.

Chrysler and AMC were working on a "contract assembly" deal for AMC to build the M-body vehicles (Chrysler 5th Avenue, Plymouth Gran Fury and this Dodge Diplomat) for Chrysler in Kenosha and save thousands of jobs. But when the American Motors Corporation acquisition was announced, the plans started to unfurl and the jobs soon disappeared.

An AMC Board Meeting at the then-uncompleted Bramalea Assembly Plant just outside of Toronto, Canada. Hardly the rich mahogany one thinks of concerning corporate board rooms. From left and clockwise, board members Jean Marc Lepeu, Joe Cappy, José Dedeurwaerder, Roy Chapin Jr., Andy Sage, Pierre Semerena, John Tierney and Allan Chapin.

Steve Harris, an up-and-coming PR executive, was Cappy's lead and had arranged a luncheon at the famous Fish Shanty in Los Angeles where he walked Cappy through the "mouth of the whale" front door to appear before the 'L.A. Economic Club." According to Harris, the "crowd could be in the hundreds. But it was just five people." On the "red-eye flight" back to Detroit, Cappy asked Harris, "What the hell went wrong?" Harris replied, "Joe, you're only as good as your draw!" Joe Cappy would change that in short order.

(left to right) In 1984, then-Renault Chairman Bernard Hanon joined Joe Cappy and AMC chief engineer Francois Castaing in the Arizona desert to give the Chairman a taste of "Jeepness." Hanon was a very popular figure but stepped down in the spring of 1985, replaced by Georges Besse.

AMC's second-in-command PR Guy Steve Harris took to the skies while on a press preview for American Motors. Later, the sky would be the limit as he became Chrysler's PR chief and later led PR at General Motors. He mentored Jason Vines and Tony Cervone at Chrysler, and for a short time in 2000, Harris was the head of PR at General Motors, while Vines and Cervone were the PR chiefs of Ford Motor Company and Chrysler, respectively.

Pete Guptill, new General Manager U.S. Sales executive made a point that CEO José Dedeurwaerder could finally understand regarding the sudden fall-off of sales of the Renault Fuego. Pete said, "Jose', the Fuego is the most attractive looking car sitting dead on the shoulder of all the highways in the country. Our dealers call the car, the NO GO, FUEGO." (Guptill is shown in Off-Road Racing gear while competing in the Baja 500 Race in Mexico)

Joe Cappy with (center) Todd Clare,
AMC's VP International Operations, and
Jesus Peon, AMC's VP Manufacturing.

As Chrysler and Renault danced for
the sale of American Motors, it was
this Renault Allure concept car, the
two-door version of the Renault
(then-Eagle) Premier, which would
never see the light of day.

AMC HQ: You can see it for miles, but because it was situated between a spider web of freeways called "Malfunction Junction," it was almost impossible to get to on the first try.

Flipping the Bird in 1987: After signing the "automotive deal of the Century" on 5th floor of Chrysler's incredibly crappy HQ in Highland Park, Michigan, Chrysler Vice-Chairman R. Steve Miller (center left), the true architect of the Chrysler's deal to buy American Motors, finally let down his "hair" and tells his friend Joe Cappy what he really thinks about the negotiations. Behind Miller is Chrysler General Counsel Dick Goodyear.

Everyone's a winner

Nobody at Chrysler loses, it's said, as AMC is swallowed

By BURT STODDARD

Chrysler Corp.'s final purchase/takeover of American Motors Corp. on Aug. 5 spawns a confusing same-day shuffle of a president, a chairman, a vice chairman and assorted vice presidents that appears to result in the demotion — at least in title — of one prominent Chrysler officer, Bennett E. Bidwell. But "that isn't functionally true," says a Chrysler spokesman.

Mr. Bidwell is moved from vice chairman of Chrysler Corp., reporting to Chrysler Chairman Lee A. Iacocca, to vice chairman of subsidiary Chrysler Motors Corp, reporting to Chrysler Motors Chairman Gerald Greenwald.

What happened, the spokesman adds, is that Mr. Bidwell, who played a key role in negotiating the AMC acquisition, is "needed at Chrysler Motors to help fold AMC in; he's a great marketer you know." At Chrysler Motors, Mr. Bidwell will be responsible to Mr. Greenwald for sales and service activities, including the highly important task of marketing the new Jeep/Eagle line of former AMC products.

Additionally, Mr. Bidwell remains on the 6-member Chrysler executive committee chaired by Mr. Iacocca "so you can see he's still right in the midst of things," adds the spokesman.

Supporting that is the fact that among the three vice presidents now reporting to

Mr. Bidwell is Joseph E. Cappy, the former AMC president and chief executive officer, who comes into Chrysler as a group vice president in charge of "advertising, merchandising, and brand and dealer marketing" for Jeep/Eagle and to head a "transition team" of former AMC executives who'll coordinate the integration of AMC into Chrysler Motors.

Two other top-level AMC executives brought immediately to Chrysler with Mr. Cappy are François J. Castaing, who was AMC's group vice president-product and quality, as Chrysler Motors' vice president-Jeep and truck engineering; and John P. Tierney, from AMC's vice president-chief financial officer to chairman of Chrysler Financial Corp. (CFC).

Mr. Tierney's appointment startles some, too, as he replaces Robert S. Miller atop CFC, Chrysler's car-financing arm that now has diversified into leasing, commercial and consumer loans and other money services. Mr. Miller, who led the negotiations with AMC's former controlling owner, Regie Renault, remains next to Mr. Iacocca as the only vice chairman of Chrysler Corp. and an executive committee member, but loses the CFC title.

Less title is called more for Mr. Miller, too. "Steve Miller has got CFC rolling with a plan well into the future," the spokesman says. "Now, with a person of John

Tierney's ability to carry on, he (Mr. Miller) can concentrate in other, more urgent, areas." Mr. Miller's vice chairmanship covers Chrysler's controller, treasury, internal audit, general counsel and tax activities.

The AMC-purchase shuffle seems to support chances of both Mr. Miller, 47 years old in November, and Mr. Greenwald, 52 this month, to succeed Mr. Iacocca, who will be 63 in October '89.

If anything, Mr. Greenwald's star is more enhanced because the changes mean that three members of the executive committee now report to him on an operating basis, namely Mr. Bidwell, Chrysler Motors President Harold K. Sperlich and Robert A. Lutz, one of four Chrysler Motors executive vice presidents. Some had thought Mr. Greenwald was hurt by the revelations in June that test mileage had been wiped off new car odometers at Chrysler plants — actions that Mr. Iacocca called "stupid" and publicly apologized for.

While Mr. Iacocca hailed the three moving from AMC — Mr. Cappy, Mr. Castaing and Mr. Tierney — who help Chrysler cover the engineering, marketing and financing of the Jeep/Eagle integration, it appears there will be few, if any more, high-level transferees.

To handle the other major area, manufacturing, seven Chrysler Motors executives are given enlarged roles within the existing manufacturing setup run by Richard E. Dauch, executive vice president-manufacturing.

The seven include Ronald L. Stewart, who moves from vice-president-Car and

The AMC-bolstered Chrysler Corp. "team" includes (from left) Mr. Sperlich, Mr. Greenwald, Mr. Tierney, Mr. Cappy, Mr. Iacocca, Mr. Castaing, Mr. Lutz, Mr. Bidwell and Mr. Miller.

9·87 WARD'S Auto World

Automotive magazine *Ward's* story about the deal said it all.
(Reprinted by permission from WardsAuto.)

Joe Cappy, today, with a
bronze of a man reading _The
Detroit News_ signifying the
importance of Chrysler's
purchase of American Motors.
The bronze resides in the
Grand Circus Park People
Mover station in downtown
Detroit. The headline reads,
"Chrysler, AMC Approve
Merger."

At the signing of the deal, members of the Titan Project, the codename for
Chrysler's acquisition of AMC, met with AMC's top leaders. (Front Row,
left to right) AMC Board Secretary John Sheridan, AMC CFO John Tierney,
Joe Cappy, Chrysler CFO R. Steve Miller and Chrysler's General Counsel
Dick Goodyear. (Back Row, left to right all Chrysler except where noted)
Commercial Attorney Geoff Hass, Asst. General Counsel William O'Brien,
Controller James Donlon, (Unidentified person), Treasurer Tom Capo,
Debovoise & Plimpton Attorney Paul Wilson, General Manager Mergers and
Acquisitions Ralph Sarotte and Attorney Howard Hill.

The legendary engineer Francois Castaing first gained notice in Renault's Formula One program and later at American Motors. He brought his "platform team" approach of vehicle development to Chrysler and it transformed the company.

FRANCOIS J. CASTAING

The 1988 Eagle Premier was the first product from the new plant in Canada. The sedan was supposed to be launched in the fall of 1987, but electronic glitches caused a delay until the following spring. A decent car, but it became "dead car walking" when Chrysler decided to make a Dodge version of the vehicle and the Dodge dealers pummeled the tiny Eagle dealers. It was "badge engineering" at its worst.

Chrysler CEO Lee Iacocca called the original design of the 1990 Eagle Talon "horsey" and so the designers went back to work and changed the look. When they showed Iacocca the new rendition he asked "what the hell happened to the other one?" The designers responded, "You called it horsey," to which Iacocca barked, "yeah, like a (Ford) Mustang. I loved it." Hundreds of thousands of dollars had been wasted because nobody had the balls to ask Iacocca what he meant.

The late General George C. Marshall, the man who later spear-headed the U.S.-led rebuilding of war-torn Europe with "The Marshall Plan," called the original Jeep vehicle, the MB41, "America's greatest contribution to modern warfare."

The first "civilian" Jeep vehicle, the CJ2A, was designed primarily for farm work. It would soon spawn several generations of the quintessential Jeep, known today as the Jeep Wrangler.

The granddaddy of the Jeep line-up, the Grand Wagoneer had customer demographics that mirrored Mercedes Benz. Many of its loyal customers were so well-heeled, they paid cash for their Grand Wagoneer.

The 1987 Wrangler was the quintessential Jeep vehicle with direct ties to the original Jeep military vehicle. This photo was shot in California prior to the vehicle's launch. Behind the wheel was the AMC-turned-Chrysler PR guy John McCandless. But, when McCandless took a job at Toyota, the Chrysler PR staff "air-brushed" him out of the photo.

On August 5, 1987, Chrysler Chairman CEO Lee Iacocca got his baby, the Jeep brand. Chrysler (now Fiat Chrysler Automobiles) has been the steward of the brand longer than any of the other predecessor owners, including its creator, Willys.

Created by American Motors engineers prior to Chrysler's purchase, the Jeep ZJ Concept would become one of the most successful and profitable vehicles in automotive history as the Jeep Grand Cherokee.

The new Jeep Grand Cherokee literally crashed the party at the 1992 Detroit Motor Show. Chrysler Vice Chairman Bob Lutz drove the vehicle from its home, the Jefferson Avenue Assembly Plant, up the stairs and through the glass of Cobo Hall. Riding shotgun was Detroit Mayor Coleman A. Young. The stunt would be the start of Chrysler's Detroit Motor Show dominance.

Note: All photos, except where indicated, are used with permission from Fiat Chrysler Automobiles.

Chapter 17
Lights, Cameras…In-Action!

Jerry Sloan, Vice President of Public Relations and his number one assistant, Steve Harris, were more than PR specialists to Joe Cappy. They were alter egos and extremely close and trusted counselors. He valued their opinions and sought their advice on a host of issues and problems. So when they came to him shortly after he was appointed President and CEO with any idea, he always listened. Of course, not all of their suggestions were assured winners.

Sloan and Harris came to Cappy with a "wonderful opportunity" to address the Los Angeles Economic Club, one of the largest business clubs in the country with a membership of 10,000 people. Telling this group the AMC story would be a "home run." Sloan added, "You've got to do it." Cappy was intrigued and checked his schedule, but he was booked solid. Harris said, "Let me study this and the airline schedules as well."

Harris found a flight that would get into LAX in time to make a luncheon since the meeting location was just outside the busy airport. Then, by taking a "red-eye" flight back to Detroit, Cappy could make his 8:00 a.m. meeting in Detroit the next morning.

Cappy still wasn't sold on the idea, but Sloan and Harris continued to stress the high visibility of this group of business leaders. When Cappy found out the meeting was actually an off-shoot of the main body of the club, he asked what Harris's estimate was for the actual audience size. Harris said he expected 200 to 300 members. With that number, Cappy enthusiastically gave the go ahead to proceed.

Upon arriving in L.A., Harris rented a car and he and Cappy headed off to the luncheon. Harris also had a slide tray that Cappy would use to talk from. (For the younger readers, a slide tray includes tiny little photos of charts and products that you put on a "slide projector," a machine – oh, never mind. Think YouTube, a single-photo at a time, or a collection of "selfies.") Ahem.

Harris had a minor problem in finding the meeting place, but finally found the location and parked. Cappy got out of the car and said, "Steve, where is it?" looking for some type of large hall or convention center. Harris pointed out a restaurant with a front doorway shaped into the mouth of a whale. Cappy was shaken and stirred. "You brought me out here for this!" Harris replied: "Calm down, Joe, this place has large meeting rooms in the back of the restaurant."

Like Jonah, Joe Cappy entered the mouth of the whale, um, door with Harris leading the way. Cappy remained skeptical, but as the duo walked through the restaurant, sure enough, in the back were a series of meeting rooms. Cappy's eyes moved room-to-room as he followed his PR man Harris, and then stopped when he spotted a room filled with about 200 people – all women.

"Joe, that's not our room," Harris said, just as Cappy noticed the meeting sign: Planned Parenthood. Cappy continued to follow Harris who turned the corner at the end of the corridor. In a flash, Harris turned around and rushed toward Cappy saying, "Joe, now take it easy."

Cappy pushed past Harris and went around the corner and saw a meeting room with a sign for the L.A. Economic Club. The room was small and set up for a table of eight – not 80, not 800. Eight. A starting baseball team would more than fill the room. Harris and Cappy looked at each other like someone had told them cars had run over their dogs. Cappy looked at Harris: "Forget the projector, I'll pass the slides around by hand."

When the L.A. Economic Club "members" arrived, the singular eight-top table had one open seat. Lunch was served and Cappy began to spin his glorious story of American Motors for the five people who hadn't heard it before. Harris, who actually would become a genuine PR guru at Chrysler and later General Motors, was merely doing his best to stay awake.

With the "L.A. Economic Club" luncheon over, on the way back to LAX for the "red-eye" flight to Detroit, Cappy asked Harris, "What the hell went wrong?" Harris replied, "Joe, you're only as good as your draw!" Joe Cappy would change that in short time.

Chapter 18
The Crazy Americans

The U.S. automotive market has always been extremely competitive, beginning with product and continuing with pricing – often pricing similar-type vehicles within pennies or dollars of one another. When rebates directly to consumers began, the marketplace once again responded with copycat programs and similar cash payments to buyers. Think of Lee Iacocca's famous line in the Chrysler commercials: "Buy a car, get a check."

In an effort to induce consumers to buy new vehicles at a time when interest rates were high, General Motors in September 1986 introduced low interest rate financing to the public in an attempt at triggering vigorous Labor Day weekend sales with a 2.9 percent interest rate on three-year loans.

Less than a week later, Ford Motor Company and Chrysler Corporation jumped into the fray. Ford matched GM's 2.9 percent rate on 36-month contracts. Chrysler went one better than GM and Ford and tossed out a 2.4 percent interest rate on 24-month loans. Since more consumers would likely opt for three-year financing to keep monthly payments lower than a two-year deal, Chrysler's industry low 2.4 percent rate was merely a marketing ploy: they could get people into the showroom with the lowest rate available knowing most customers would choose to keep their monthly payment lower. Indeed, it was a ploy, a brilliant ploy!

The game was on! Smaller import players like Peugeot of America jumped in offering a 2.2 percent interest rate on two of their models. AMC was in a bit of a bind. Its financing arm was not adequately capitalized, and actually was run as an offshoot of Chrysler Financial. Responding with a matching program could be very costly for AMC. However, AMC knew it couldn't stay on the sidelines, since the consumers were ramping up their purchases to take advantage of the below-market interest rates.

Joe Cappy called a meeting with Geoffrey Banks, director of AMC Credit, and Peter Guptill, VP of Sales and Marketing. AMC needed to announce an interest rate program to keep its dealer body competitive. Cappy requested that Banks and Guptill go look at alternatives and costs for an AMC program as quickly as possible. Banks and Guptill returned in short order with a response that would take the nation by storm. The program they returned with was ZERO PERCENT FINANCING. In a game of "how low can you go?" zero was it! It was affordable for AMC due to its construction, taking a page right out of Chrysler's playbook, or Chrysler's "ploybook?" The AMC deal was zero percent interest on 12-month loans.

The AMC team knew that consumers who might finance a car for only 12 months normally had the cash to purchase the car outright, and never bothered with financing their new vehicle purchase. Well-heeled customers that bought high-end Jeep vehicles, like the Grand Wagoneer, often times writing a check for the entire price of the vehicle. The rates AMC proposed for 24- and 36-month financing were, in turn, slightly higher than the GM, Ford and Chrysler programs. Overall, the new AMC interest rate program was the lowest cost program – for the manufacturer – in the industry.

But, here was the magic: American Motors had an interest rate program the consumers perceived as the best in the country. Zero percent said it all. The media went wild. Phones rang off the hook in the PR department with hundreds of calls from radio and newspaper reporters asking for interviews with AMC executives. Local television stations and network affiliates wanted face-to-face interviews. CNN TV reporter Robert Vito came to AMC's HQ in Southfield, Michigan – American Center – with a camera crew for an interview, followed by the other networks. The *Larry King* radio show promised an hour of talk show time if Joe Cappy went to his radio studio in Washington, D.C., for an interview.

The hysteria reached "epic" levels in the marketplace. Across the country, AMC dealers were swamped with potential buyers. Dealers were passing out numbers, similar to a meat counter at a grocery store, as to who would be waited on next. Some buyers sat in vehicles they intended to buy and wouldn't get out until a salesperson called their number. In a matter of ten days, dealer inventories were totally depleted.

Management euphoria inside American Center, however, quickly evaporated when Cappy received a call from Renault HQ in Paris. On the line, Jean-Marc Lepeu, sales and marketing chief José Dedeurwaerder's chief of staff, told Cappy Renault's Chairman, Georges Besse, wanted to see Cappy the next day in Paris. Lepeu laid it out: all of France was in an uproar over the Americans at AMC giving away the French Government's money in such a wild and undisciplined manner.

Cappy suggested Lepeu contact John Tierney, AMC's CFO, to secure the financial cost analysis to understand how AMC's interest rate program costs were lower than all of its competitors. Apparently, José Dedeurwaerder was out of the country and Chairman Besse was unable to contact him. Cappy made immediate plans to fly out that night to Paris for his meeting with Besse.

Upon arrival in Paris, Cappy was escorted to a location where Besse was meeting with French Government officials. Besse's meeting was on a coffee break, and Lepeu met Cappy at the door to escort him to where Besse was standing. On the way, Lepeu informed Cappy he had gotten all of the AMC financial costs and had reviewed them with Besse, along with the fact that AMC's previously dire, huge dealer inventory problem had evaporated as a result of the wildly successful program.

Besse shook Cappy's hand. Besse's hand was as dry as the Sahara, while Cappy's hand, by his own description, was "a bit clammy." Besse did not mince words: the new AMC interest rate program was a very clever move. He thanked Cappy, said "keep up the good work," and returned to his meeting with the French Government. The meeting lasted less than two minutes. Joe Cappy had flown 3,941 miles on no sleep for an "Atta boy." As he boarded the plane for the flight back to Detroit, he was jet-lagged but on top of the world; figuratively at that point and literally as the plane crossed the Atlantic Ocean.

Back in Detroit, the next day it was off to Washington, D.C., for an appearance on the hugely popular *Larry King Show*. Before the radio show began, Cappy had called his mother to tell her to listen to the program that night since he was going to be on the show for an entire hour. If you had good news to share, Larry King was about as good as you could get as he had a reputation for allowing his guests to tell their story. While it was "his" show, he always allowed guests who listened to call in and ask questions. For Cappy's appearance, all of the callers were positive and Cappy was able to answer their questions easily.

Near the end of the hour, King took a call from Tampa, Florida. Once the caller started to ask her question for Joe Cappy, he quickly recognized the voice – it was his sister who lived in Tampa close to their mother. Cappy worried his whole hour of "greatness" on the ***Larry King Show*** was about to be destroyed.

But, his sister Grayce asked a question about her, as a teenager, working for her father's business in Wisconsin. Without skipping a beat, Cappy answered the question, praised the father and daughter, and got the hell outta Dodge.

Even with all of the great news, Cappy had one very unpleasant interview. AMC PR chief Jerry Sloan had a request for a Cappy interview from Detroit's ABC affiliate, WXYZ, with Bill Bonds, the most controversial yet most-watched news anchor in Detroit. The only catch was Cappy would have to go to WXYZ's studio to do the interview. All the other networks and their affiliates had been coming to AMC's headquarters to interview Cappy, so he was reluctant to take the time to run to their studio—even though it was literally just minutes away from his office.

But his PR chief kept pushing Cappy, saying he shouldn't pass up the opportunity. Cappy finally acquiesced and he and Sloan rushed off to get on the early evening newscast at the ABC affiliate's studio. Upon arrival, things started to unravel for the dynamic duo. Cappy was asked to sit on a stool in the lobby of the studio where they placed a hearing bud in his ear and clipped a mike on his jacket. Cappy looked at Sloan and said if he couldn't sit across the anchor desk from Bill Bonds, face to face, he wanted to leave.

Sloan quieted Cappy down and again said the opportunity was too good to pass up. Cappy remained concerned because Bill Bonds was an acerbic fellow who, rumored abounded, drank heavily and had gotten into bar fights and other mishaps over the years. It was most likely the reason he had so many viewers, as it was sort of like waiting to see a train wreck on live TV.

But, Cappy had been interviewed all day long on AMC's zero percent financing program and believed he could handle any question Bonds tossed at him. Cappy was watching a small television set, about 30 feet from Bonds but on the other side of a wall, as the newscast got underway. After about ten minutes and five commercials, Bonds introduced Cappy as President and CEO of American Motors.

Bonds then asked, "Tell me Mr. Cappy, why do the Japanese cars have better quality than the American cars?"

It was a quiet ride back to the AMC offices and no one was quieter than Jerry Sloan.

Chapter 19
Those Crazy French!

When two cultures merge, plus two nationalities, regardless of how much effort is made to make the new combined entities function smoothly, difficulties can arise – sometimes on purpose.

Joe Cappy was invited to attend a worldwide meeting of Renault sales executives in Nice, France. He asked two of his top sales and marketing executives to join him: Peter Guptill, VP of Sales and Marketing, and Marty Levine, General Marketing Manager.

The Renault meeting was held in the Nice Convention Center and was conducted entirely in French, which was complete "Greek" to the trio of Americans. Cappy and his crew wore headphones and listened to a translator convert the comments of various speakers into English – albeit, a beat or two after the speaker's actual words. All of the slides were in French as well.

The topics covered included discussions on warranty problems and technical issues on products not sold in the U.S. market; car and truck parts distribution around the world in countries like Algiers, Morocco, Turkey, and French Congo. There was no mention of New York, Los Angeles, or Gary, Indiana. In a darkened auditorium and listening to a translator on topics you have no interest in is tiring at best.

It was a long morning session, but then came a lunch break, along with the food were bottles of fine French wine and baguettes of bread. Cappy's crew imbibed the wine as though they were Frenchmen accustomed to drinking wine at lunch. It was a bad move. Soon, however, the entire group reconvened and the presentations continued.

Staying alert and attentive after lunch and wine was nearly impossible. Finally, around 4:00 p.m., a break was called. Cappy struggled to find an exit to the outdoors. Guptill and Levine were close behind and all were blinking at the bright sunlight and warm weather. It was a spectacular day outside in Nice. Marty Levine approached Cappy and Guptill and barked out, "I don't know about you guys, but I'm ready to talk! I can't take any more of this torture."

Renault regularly scheduled production and allocation meetings in Paris for worldwide distribution. Their U.S. counterparts were included in these meetings most of the time. A particular meeting was scheduled; this time not in Paris but rather at the R5 (Renault LeCar) Plant in northwest France, close to the Belgium border. The idea was to bring plant management and sales and marketing people together for exposure to all disciplines of the company. The selected location was not convenient for an AMC executive flying in from the United States, but the idea behind the meeting seemed legitimate and actually helpful.

The meeting was billed as a major meeting, so Peter Guptill decided to attend himself. Having served in the military, Guptill was ready for any transportation challenges. To insure his timely arrival without asking for any assistance from Renault personnel, Guptill flew into Brussels, Belgium, one day early. He rented a car, checked into a hotel, and despite overnight jet lag, secured a map and decided to pre-trip his drive to the plant for the next day's meeting.

The route took Guptill on a long and winding road through villages and the countryside to find the plant. He was glad he did because it would have been daunting to arrive on time the next morning without the pre-trip experience. The round-trip took most of the day and Guptill stopped for dinner before heading back to his hotel around 9:30 p.m. that night.

Upon entering his room, Guptill found an envelope on the floor with a message from his secretary in Detroit informing him that the meeting had been moved to Paris for the next morning at 7:30 a.m. Guptill had usually spoken his piece on issues defending the AMC contributions at these meetings. Changing the location of the meeting with no notice and with him in Brussels all-but assured his absence at the next day's meeting in Paris, and a meeting with fewer objections from a "pesky" American.

But, the U.S. Navy didn't raise wimps. Guptill called the airlines, but there were no flights that evening to Paris.

By this time it was 10:30 p.m. and no alternatives. Guptill packed his bag and went to the lobby to check out. After some discussion, the hotel agreed to charge him for just one night. He attempted to contact his rental car company without success. So Guptill got his rental car and laid out a route to Paris, about 200 miles away. Without a hotel reservation in Paris, and never having driven in Europe before – except for his pre-trip to the plant earlier in the day – it was anchors aweigh.

Driving out of Brussels in the dead of night, it appeared every truck, semi-tractor trailer, and delivery van in Europe was on the road with him. Apparently, they discouraged commercial traffic in the daytime and it all convened at night on the highway. Everything went fine until he reached a tollbooth just over the French border. It was pre-Euro Europe and Guptill had just a few Belgium francs, some U.S. dollars, but no French francs. The tollbooth operator was extremely helpful: "Too bad, get out of line." At least that's what Guptill thought the Frenchman said. What to do?

Turning around, Guptill spotted a truck stop and went to get change for his U.S. currency. The cashier shook her head: No! The Navy vet shook his head and thought: "You're welcome for saving your ass from Hitler!" But then he got an idea and got into the cafeteria line, grabbed a Coke and a baguette, took a big bite and a gulp and returned to the cashier. He gave her a $20 bill and shrugged his shoulders, as if to say, "That's all I have." She gave him a dirty look and handed over about $9 worth of French francs. It was the most he'd ever paid for a pop and a piece of bread, but he was not missing the meeting in Paris and he would explain it to his boss Joe Cappy when he handed in his business expense report.

Guptill got back in his rental and squeezed between two huge trucks in the tollbooth line. He felt like a rowboat between two aircraft carriers. It was now 2:00 a.m., but Guptill had "a Coke and a smile." Arriving in Paris, he parked illegally in front of a hotel, got a room, showered, dressed and left for the meeting at the Renault headquarters. At about 7:35 a.m., he walked into a full meeting room and said, "Bonjour." Jaws dropped and some key people must have thought, "How the hell did he get here?"

Guptill got to a lot of places as AMC's sales chief. In London, Guptill was preparing to host an award trip the next day for dealers for a photographic safari in Kenya when he received a phone call from Joe Cappy. Calls from headquarters are rarely a good sign, and it wasn't now – just as he was getting ready to depart on a once-in-a-lifetime trip with his wife and a number of AMC's best dealers.

Cappy explained that Renault intended to discontinue production of the disastrous Renault Fuego during the next production cycle and was holding a meeting in Paris to determine the final allocation of Fuego production worldwide. Cappy strongly believed that AMC's interests needed to be served at this meeting as AMC had "experience" with "Renault math" as to a fair share allocation of a slow-moving product.

Guptill said goodbye Kenya, goodbye dealers, hello Heathrow, and off to Paris he went to attend the Fuego "build-out" meeting. The meeting began with a review of past and future production to the end. All of this review was routine and expected. Then came the crux of the meeting: How many units was AMC going to have to accept of the build-out production?

When the numbers were put up on the screen, Guptill was stunned at the number allocated to AMC. He quickly protested and asked for justification of the allocation. The reply was that it was based upon sales. Guptill quickly calculated that AMC had sold more Fuegos in the United States and Canada than the rest of Renault combined, including the home country of France.

Guptill's head exploded. He had been ridiculed by Renault management, by then-AMC CEO José Dedeurwaerder, and even his current boss Joe Cappy, for doing such a "lousy" sales job on Fuego for years, a vehicle that, due to quality problems, became a total flop. Even his dedication to the Renault brand had been questioned. So now he finds out that his sales team had outsold the world?

Guptill gathered himself before he told the group that he thought AMC had done enough, and it was time for other markets, including France, to step-up. AMC had enough dealer inventory of the Fuego, along with several hundred vehicles still sitting in the ports, to last them throughout the build-out period...and beyond. The other market representatives were mostly silent and sheepish while Guptill stood firm. The final result was the U.S. received a token more Fuegos with the bulk distributed among the other markets. Guptill never made it to Kenya and probably never will, but it was good for AMC that he had made his way to Paris.

Chapter 20
Icebergs Ahead

In a transaction the size of the sale of American Motors and its diamond-in-the-rough Jeep brand, there are myriad issues to resolve when both parties have different positions that many times are deal breakers. The cry, "Icebergs Dead Ahead," properly reflected some of the major issues confronting both Chrysler Corporation and Renault and stood in the way of their secret negotiations in the fall of 1986.

However, two critical issues immediately became apparent. The first was Chrysler agreeing to purchase AMC's entire organization, financial responsibilities, and accept its dealer body, as Renault was planning to abandon the U.S. marketplace, just like the Baltimore Colts pulled out of town and relocated to Indianapolis in the dark of night two years earlier.

The second issue was Chrysler agreeing on a satisfactory financial payment to Renault for the purchase of American Motors. In reality, Chrysler really was only interested in buying the Jeep brand, product line, manufacturing facilities, and engineering team – masters in the art of four-wheel drive. But, it was obvious fairly early in discussions between the parties that the "just Jeep" position was a non-starter for Renault. To get Jeep, the French made clear, all of AMC was going to have to be part of the deal. So, Iacocca said, "Let's look at the whole company."

Certainly there were a lot of outstanding people at AMC – many had succeeded at other car companies, like Joe Cappy, and many had excelled in other industries. On top of that, some of the AMC/Jeep dealers could push metal with the best in the business.

But the cost to acquire AMC as a whole seemed enormous for a Chrysler Corporation less than five years from death's door of near-bankruptcy. Chrysler management knew, for example, that they would have to provide an AMC/Jeep dealer network with a family of cars to replace the existing and planned Renault car lines that the AMC dealer network was then selling with limited success, with the exception of the Renault Alliance.

In addition, Chrysler did not have the capital to rebadge their Chrysler, Dodge, and Plymouth cars and Dodge trucks as AMC vehicles, or develop and produce a new line of cars to compliment the Jeep Cherokee and Wrangler vehicles for the AMC dealers. But, Chrysler Corporation was not going to be able to pick and choose.

Early in 1986, this would be the conundrum Chrysler negotiators would face over the next six months in order to get access to AMC's jewel – Jeep.

Offer after offer after offer had been presented to Renault and not accepted. Chrysler's top sales executive and confidante of CEO Lee Iacocca, Ben Bidwell, and

Chrysler's lead banker concluded that Renault didn't want to sell American Motors. At least not to Chrysler Corporation. In Bidwell's mind, the deal was going nowhere and Chrysler shouldn't waste time and energy chasing it anymore, unless there was a sudden, strong indication from Renault that they were willing to make a deal.

Steve Miller, Chrysler's financial maestro who was the brains behind the company's negotiations with the U.S. Government to keep Chrysler afloat a few years earlier, was more optimistic and wanted to get more bankers involved. His rationale to the bankers: help us pull off this deal and it is a huge payday for you. Miller believed the deal was far from dead and kept plugging away. But the added bankers kept setting up meetings after meetings with little or no results. Bidwell continued to complain that "there was no deal there."

Time went on. More offers for the purchase of AMC were made and all were rejected. No combination of terms seemed acceptable to Renault. What's more, if a deal could actually be reached, there were still considerable icebergs in the water ahead that Chrysler had to navigate with the Titanic of the auto industry, AMC.

Icebergs? If an agreement in principle was reached and announced, it would be up to Joe Cappy, AMC President and CEO, to keep the AMC organization working together during the due diligence period, to ensure that value would be there for Chrysler when the deal closed. Cappy would also want to protect his people who were loyal to him and the company, successfully integrate the merger of AMC into Chrysler to preserve as many positions for the AMC staff as possible, while still keeping the organization viable and doing business in the event an insurmountable problem arose during the due diligence period. Leaving this last critical part of the acquisition in AMC's hands was a major risk Chrysler would have to take. However, Chrysler was so anxious to get Jeep they agreed to accept this risk and work on the final details during the follow-up negotiations with Renault and subsequent discussions with Cappy, provided a deal was made.

The talks continued at this point without any knowledge by Joe Cappy, President and CEO of AMC, of the potential and the icebergs ahead. It was simply the "boys" at Chrysler Corporation and the top dogs at Renault in Paris. That would change. Quickly.

Chapter 21
Ship it Where?

In the late fall of 1986, José Dedeurwaerder, now Renault's Worldwide Sales and Marketing VP, called AMC CEO Joe Cappy and asked him to ship to Atlantic City, New Jersey, the fiberglass styling prototype of AMC's next major new vehicle just one year away from production in Canada – the Renault Premier. The Premier model was the first new vehicle to be developed in the United States jointly by AMC and Renault, and produced in North America in a new plant under construction in Bramalea, Ontario, Canada. It was AMC's most critical new product, and its most closely guarded secret.

Cappy was puzzled: "Ship it where?"

José "explained" because Renault was seeking to contract "an insurance policy on volume," he wanted to get an estimate on how many Renault Premiers could be sold by Renault's worldwide distribution system. He was "having all of Renault's worldwide sales managers come to the United States to view the styling property. Having the property on the East Coast in Atlantic City would allow them to arrive in New York City, view the property, and depart much sooner than continuing on to the AMC Tech Center in a deteriorating section of Detroit. It would also eliminate a great number of Renault executives from crawling all over the tech center creating even more rumors."

The above paragraph, and ones to follow, contain many statements in quotations, not because they were actual quotes, but because they were complete bullshit in retrospect.

On the surface, and at the time, the rationale José Dedeurwaerder presented seemed sound and Cappy asked for the date and time the styling property should arrive in Atlantic City and at which hotel. He also asked whom José wanted to attend from AMC. José said no one was really needed since he would be the one describing the styling property to the "Renault" attendees.

José issued Cappy a caveat: the shipping must be carried out with a maximum of security within AMC. Prototype cars daily drove around the roads and highways of Metro Detroit with camouflage disguising their styling. José was treating the Premier as if it was a secret weapon he was sharing with the "enemy".

Nonetheless, per the orders from Renault, the Premier fiberglass styling property was shipped and returned without incident for the showing to the "Renault worldwide salesforce."

Cappy would soon enough learn that the Renault Premier property had been sent to Atlantic City for a private car show for Chrysler executives, including CEO Lee Iacocca. The real purpose was to see how the Premier, still in development and a year away from production, stacked up to current and future Chrysler products, which had also been shipped to Atlantic City.

Showing an advanced styling property to the competition was absolutely unthinkable – especially since no letter of intent or sales agreement had been signed. However, doing so showed Renault would stop at nothing to unload AMC. Since Chrysler had their future products there as well, it could be argued it was reciprocal, except Renault was not a competitor with Chrysler in the United States, and not a single American Motors executive was present. Renault wore its desperation on its sleeves.

Despite José Dedeurwaerder's reasoning to Cappy behind the shipment of the styling property, Joe was disturbed, thanks to the growing Chrysler/AMC rumors circulating throughout his company from a variety of sources. Finally, Cappy had had enough and decided to go right to a source he knew would give him a straight answer: Lee Iacocca's top sales and marketing executive, Ben Bidwell.

Joe Cappy had reported directly to Bidwell at the Ford Motor Company and had an excellent relationship with him. In fact, when Cappy got his COO assignment at American Motors, Bidwell wrote a letter of congratulations mentioning he had trained both CEO Paul Tippett and Joe Cappy. He went further to add, "If I read the papers right, you're (Cappy) even going to run the assembly plants! As they say in America, anything's possible."

Cappy called Bidwell and asked him directly: "What the hell is going on between Chrysler and Renault?" Cappy's boss, José, wouldn't tell him anything, and he felt like the legendary Gordie Howe did when the "old" owners of the Detroit Red Wings said "they were giving him the 'mushroom treatment' – throw him in a dark room, and occasionally open the door and throw more shit on him."

Cappy asked about the possible, clandestine deal. He was not totally in the dark. Bidwell's response to Cappy's question confirmed Joe's feeling: "You are trying to peer into the darkness, trying to figure out if there are consenting adults out there, and what were they doing to each other."

Bidwell asked if Cappy could come to his house on Sunday at 11 a.m. in the toney suburb of Detroit, Bloomfield Hills. Bidwell said he would take one car out of his two-car garage and leave the garage door open. Cappy was to pull in and close the garage door. Bidwell didn't want anyone to see a Renault Alliance parked in front of his house.

Cappy arrived at Bidwell's home as scheduled and Bidwell met him as he pulled into the garage. It was a scene out of *All the President's Men*. Cappy wondered if Bidwell would be his "Deep Throat." Bidwell invited

Cappy into his living room and his wife Polly brought them coffee.

Bidwell swore Cappy to absolute secrecy and said that Joe could tell no one what he was going to pass on to him. Cappy agreed. Bidwell then outlined the entire process Chrysler had been going through in an attempt to buy Jeep and, unfortunately, all of AMC. Bidwell shared Chrysler wasn't confident a deal could be reached with Renault Chairman Besse for its 46.1 percent ownership stake in American Motors – but it wasn't for lack of trying by Chrysler.

Chrysler, at the time, had its own issues. They included an incredibly aging product line, no sleek midsize model to go up against the uber successful Ford Taurus, no domestic four-wheel-drive vehicle in the up-and-coming and soon-to-be-explosive SUV market where Jeep was entrenched, and not enough manufacturing capacity. With AMC, Chrysler would get help in each of these areas, including a third dealer network, albeit, maybe the weakest one.

Cappy thanked Bidwell for being so frank. But now Cappy had the problem with knowing something received in confidence he had to keep to himself. As he drove home, he thought of the problem the British had in World War II when they broke the German Enigma code. The British were reluctant to warn certain populated areas in advance knowing the German bombers were going to strike those areas, for fear the Germans would realize their code had been broken.

One other thought struck Joe Cappy: what side of this deal was he supposed to be on?

Jesus.

Events heated up within weeks in the fall of 1986, as Chrysler's interest increased while pressure from the French Government squeezed Renault to shed AMC. The discussions progressed to a point of planned direct negotiations between a small team from each side. Chrysler's team was comprised of Jim Donlon, VP of Finance; Dick Goodyear, VP of Legal Staff, and Ralph Sarotte, General Manager of the M&A Automotive Group, as well as several others.

They were invited by Renault Chairman Besse's representatives to fly to Paris and meet with a team from Renault to plan and negotiate the actual agreement in principle to complete the purchase of AMC from Renault by Chrysler. The team flew first to New York City to update Chrysler's Board of Directors, who were having their monthly meeting, and then would proceed directly to Paris to begin the negotiations.

The night before the Chrysler board meeting, Renault Chairman Besse's representative called to say that Besse asked for a few more days to think about the deal before negotiations could begin. As a result, the Chrysler team didn't present to the Chrysler board and returned to Detroit to await a follow-up call from Renault.

Then, days later, Friday, November 17, 1986, Renault Chairman Georges Besse was assassinated in front of his home...as his daughter watched in horror.

Renault's management, understandably, canceled the negotiation discussions with Chrysler. No one on the Chrysler team had any idea when, or if, the negotiations would be re-initiated. In fact, Chrysler's financial guru, Steve Miller, was the only optimist among the Chrysler team who thought talks could and would resume.

Miller's financial savvy had, and would, save Chrysler, and eventually American Motors. Joe Cappy knew it.

Chapter 22
I'm Not Dead Yet!

On January 1, 1987, the French Government appointed Raymond Levy, CEO of a French steel company, as Renault's new CEO. His appointment came with the strong recommendation from the French Government to sell American Motors.

Chrysler's Steve Miller suggested to his boss, CEO Lee Iacocca, that it might be the time to re-engage with Renault and its new chairman, two months after the assassination of Georges Besse. Most of the Chrysler team which had been pursuing a deal for American Motors was simply exhausted from the "chase." But not Miller. And, he had an important ally in Gerald Greenwald, the Chairman of Chrysler Motors, the vehicle-manufacturing arm of Lee Iacocca's Chrysler Corporation. Greenwald would not mince words: "We had to face the fact that we might die or retire before we could ever establish a name with even half the image of the name Jeep."

Iacocca gave Miller an edict: "You have one more chance. That's it! If this doesn't work, we move on."

Chrysler's bankers contacted Renault's financial advisors to ask if negotiations could be rescheduled. After Chairman Levy consulted with the Renault Board and the Treasurer of the French Government, he gave his advisors approval to renew talks with Chrysler. The "dead" deal due to the murder of Renault's former Chairman was about to be resuscitated.

With his negotiating team in his office, Steve Miller took the call from his Renault contacts. When he hung up the phone, he looked at his team, found his "inner Monty Python," and shouted, "It's not dead yet!"

On February 5, 1987, Raymond Levy made his first trip to the United States as Renault's Chairman to attend the Chicago Auto Show and visit the AMC Operations in suburban Detroit. But first, a pit stop. Levy stopped in New York City for a 45-minute meeting with Lee Iacocca in the Chrysler suite at the Waldorf Astoria Hotel. Neither Levy nor Iacocca were alone. Steve Miller and Ben Bidwell – whom Iacocca had designated to head the "Project Titan" acquisition team – joined the meeting, along with Chrysler Motors Chairman Gerald Greenwald. Renault's Levy had brought along José Dedeurwaerder, the former ex-pat AMC President and CEO, and Felix Rohatyn, a senior Lazard partner and an AMC director since 1980.

The message from Levy was simple: game on. Iacocca agreed and the automotive deal of the century was back on the table.

After leaving Iacocca's three-bedroom suite at the Waldorf Astoria, Levy flew to the Chicago Auto Show, along with Dedeurwaerder, and was whisked to the floor of the convention center. Levy asked AMC PR chief Jerry Sloan to see the prepared remarks of both AMC CEO Joe

Cappy, and Cappy's boss, José Dedeurwaerder. Levy proceeded to mark-up Sloan's introduction of José Dedeurwaerder, significantly changing José's title and even more significantly reducing his responsibilities. But, they were literally seconds from the start of the AMC press conference and Cappy would not see the changes in the script before the press event would begin. After he gave his prepared remarks, Cappy listened as his PR man introduced Dedeurwaerder. He noticed that Sloan had "downgraded" Dedeurwaeder's stature, but initially assumed Sloan was just doing a quicker, "Reader's Digest" version. At that moment, Cappy did not realize that when it came to Levy and Dedeurwaerder, "love was on the rocks."

Levy left Chicago and flew to Detroit on a charter flight. Two Renault ex-pat AMC executives met him at the plane and escorted him to his hotel, a short drive from the airport.

Joe Cappy wanted to ensure the Renault Chairman would be properly received in Detroit, and had called his son, Craig Cappy, the Food and Beverage Manager at the Hyatt Regency Hotel in Dearborn, Michigan, where Levy would be staying. Cappy asked his son if an "upgrade" was available for the French executive during his brief stay. The younger Cappy was smart enough to know that Thanksgiving Dinner might never be the same if he couldn't help out his old man.

At the hotel, Cappy's son took the hill and had secured for Levy the Presidential Suite—the same suite used by Ronald Reagan during the Republican National Convention in 1980 in Detroit. The suite occupied almost the entire top floor of the hotel. Walking into the suite with the Renault ex-pats, Levy exclaimed, "This suite is bigger than Lee Iacocca's suite in New York."

Aha! Another piece of the puzzle – something was going on if Levy had been in Iacocca's Waldorf Astoria suite in New York City. But, what? The Renault ex-pats passed on the new-found information to Joe Cappy the next morning, Saturday.

That same day, February 7, 1987, AMC officials delivered what they believed was the most important presentation of their lives to Renault Chairman Raymond Levy. They put on a full profit presentation and review of the company, pointing out they had turned the corner and expected to continue to make profits. Cappy said Levy was very complimentary. Cappy said, "We thought, God, he really likes us."

Unlike Sally Fields, however, Cappy didn't win an "Oscar."

One month later, Cappy and his AMC team realized they had read the tea leaves completely wrong. Levy had already decided to sell AMC to Chrysler. While all smiles during the AMC executive presentation, Levy was only looking for any negatives to bolster his decision to shed what the French Government believed was a "bottomless black hole."

Three weeks later, the talks between Renault and Chrysler resumed in the New York offices of the law firm Sullivan & Cromwell. Representing Renault were attorney Allan Chapin and Felix Rohatyn (both members of AMC's Board of Directors), Jean-Marc Lepeu, Chief of Staff for José Dedeurwaerder, the former ex-pat CFO of AMC until he returned to France a year earlier, and Paul Percie du Sert, Renault's CFO. Steve Miller and Ben Bidwell led the Chrysler team.

The discussion went over like a pregnant pole vaulter. Steve Miller laid out the myriad problems: Renault wanted more than Chrysler was willing to pay, Chrysler only wanted to buy Jeep, and Renault wanted to sell all of American Motors, as is. The discussion ended with no agreement to reconvene. So much for that. But, there was a glimmer of hope. During the meeting, Miller and Bidwell had introduced the concept of a "variable valuation" based upon future profitability of American Motors.

A week later, Iacocca, Miller, and Bidwell decided to give the deal "one more shot" following several less than unanimous executive committee discussions on Project Titan. Iacocca had reviewed negotiating parameters with the Chrysler Board's Finance Committee and then huddled with Steve Miller. Iacocca told Miller, "Go to Paris and get this thing done!" Miller immediately got on the phone to his contacts at Renault: "We're coming over." Later that day, Miller and his team boarded a corporate jet for Paris, landing the next morning, March 5, 1987. Move over jet lag, it was time to go to work.

The Chrysler team immediately spent the day working on the strategy they planned to use the next day with Renault officials. They were constantly on the phone with both Renault's negotiators and Chrysler HQ.

Then, inexplicably, Renault got squirrely, telling the Chrysler team they would not meet, nor tell the Chrysler team where they would meet if they agreed to meet, unless Chrysler agreed to certain pre-conditions. Renault was "negotiating" about how the two companies would "negotiate"? Maybe it was a French thing. Regardless, the Chrysler team rolled their eyes and "agreed" to the "pre-conditions," knowing that, in the end, they were meaningless compared to getting the deal done correctly. Renault set the meeting for the next day at the Paris office of Sullivan & Cromwell.

Leading the charge for Renault was Joe Cappy's former boss José Dedeurwaerder – when he served as AMC's President and CEO --and now Renault's Vice President for Worldwide Sales and Marketing and at the same time Vice Chairman and a director at AMC.

The deal to be negotiated was agreeing to a "variable payment" depending on the success of AMC after an acquisition by Chrysler. Renault expressed an incredibly optimistic view of the potential of AMC and insisted on an extremely high payment for the company. Chrysler had genuine concerns about the outlook for several AMC projects, and insisted on lower payments based on unknown potential results.

The first day's talks lasted until early evening. Chrysler's top lawyer, Dick Goodyear, told Steve Miller that he was going beyond Iacocca's parameters during the discussions. Miller disagreed: he was looking at the "overall" deal and was not going to nit-pick every single line item. Besides, some of the details being hammered out were far better than Iacocca sought, while some were worse.

Progress was being made, and Renault's Dedeurwaerder told the group that he believed negotiations could be concluded by noon Saturday, March 7. In his view, it was important an agreement in principle needed to be signed and announced before the opening of the New York Stock Exchange the following Monday since the financial portion of the agreement was based on the stock values of the three companies involved, Renault, Chrysler, and AMC, at of the close of business on Friday, March 6.

Both sides knew that if news of negotiations between Renault and Chrysler leaked, the agreement would change considerably as the price of one or all of the three companies' stocks would vary, and the agreement would have to be revised.

The teams met again Saturday morning, March 7. The "noon" deadline came and went as the talks continued into the evening. Still no deal, only an agreement to continue the next day, Sunday, for an effort to beat the opening bell on Wall Street Monday morning.

Chrysler had a team of financial analysts in place in its Highland Park, Michigan, headquarters tracking the negotiations and Chrysler senior management was kept up-to-date as the final details of the agreement continued to filter back. Feedback on the two companies' positions and recommended proposals for the Chrysler team in Paris were passed along for their consideration.

Finally, a breakthrough concept was established. Chrysler would pay a set compensation to Renault for "base" results. There would be the potential for extra compensation if the key AMC projects proved more successful, from a cost and profitability perspective. Therefore, the final "price" of the deal would actually not be "known" for a period of three years.

But glitches remained. Renault felt they had made the long-term investments on behalf of American Motors and should be fairly compensated. Chrysler countered that any future success would be due to added Chrysler "horsepower" applied to the projects, and they, therefore, should receive the higher rewards for success.

However, Ben Bidwell, Chrysler's top sales and marketing executive and one of three "Presidents of

Chrysler" under CEO Lee Iacocca, was so concerned about losing the deal, he recommended to Lee Iacocca and Steve Miller to "just split the difference." Bidwell's take was simple: share the rewards of success, if success is achieved. After some hand wringing, Renault agreed. Done deal.

Miller personally called Lee Iacocca to explain the final overall agreement, some parts better than hoped, and some worse. Iacocca was ecstatic, an excitement that Joe Cappy, once he learned of the deal, did not share at the time for other reasons that would become apparent and some ugliness that would develop.

The agreement in principle was signed and announced less than half an hour before the U.S. stock market opened on Monday, March 9.

Surprisingly, the payment to Renault was settled quite quickly. Chrysler wanted to get the deal done for less than $1 billion. Renault initially wanted $5 billion, but moved to $2 billion before the Chrysler team left Paris on March 10, 1987. Initially, Chrysler management believed the anxiousness of Renault management and the French Government to exit the U.S. market would give them an opportunity to grab American Motors and Jeep for a cool $1 billion, but $2 billion was a hell of a lot closer to $1 billion than Renault's initial asking price. In the end, both parties were glad it was finally over.

The final take-away: when both parties to a deal are properly motivated, it is amazing how quickly differences can be overcome.

The deal signed, the Chrysler team staggered back to the Hotel George V to get some rest. Later, as they were walking to enjoy some late winter sunshine in Paris, they had heard that Ben Bidwell had gotten ahold of Joe Cappy in his car on his way to the office to tell him about the agreement and that a letter would be hand-delivered to his office that morning. The team laughed and hoped Joe was able to keep his car on the road when he heard the news.

The next morning, the Chrysler team was booked on the Concorde to return home. On the same flight was the Renault team who were going to meet with Joe Cappy and the AMC executive team. Their faces didn't carry the same happy smiles as the Chrysler team, since both the U.S. and European media and analysts were reporting a favorable agreement for Chrysler, plus the Renault team knew that it would be a long time, if ever, before they could re-enter the U.S. marketplace, the biggest and most lucrative on the planet.

Chapter 23
Are we Sold? Liar, Liar, French Fries on Fire!

Joe Cappy and his American Motors team had moved into 1987 with too little information and declining hope for the fortunes of their company. In the last week of February 1987, an American Motors board meeting was held in Paris to provide AMC's independent directors the opportunity to meet with new Chairman Raymond Levy, installed after the assassination of Georges Besse.

The independent directors had been briefed regarding the "unusual actions and rumors" that had been taking place concerning Renault, AMC, and Chrysler. The big question in their mind was, "Are we (AMC) for sale?" The independent directors were completely in the dark, and they hoped that the new Chairman would enlighten them at the board dinner.

During cocktails and dinner, pleasant and general talk was passed. After the entrée was finished, one of the new AMC board directors, Ed Lumley, a former Cabinet Officer under former Prime Minister of Canada, Pierre Trudeau, asked Levy if he could ask him a question. Levy said, "of course."

Lumley told Renault's Chairman that the independent directors were hearing a number of rumors regarding the sale of American Motors to Chrysler. He noted that since the independent directors were responsible for the company, they were very concerned if discussions were taking place for which they were not aware. Lumley looked at Levy and asked, "Are we for sale?"

Not missing a beat, Renault's Levy pressed a button under the table and the waiters rushed in with dessert. A fellow independent director, Jack Tarver, leaned over to Lumley and said softly, "Boy, I don't think you are going to get an answer." Lumley replied, "I don't think you know us Canadians."

Undeterred, Lumley repeated his question, this time in both French and English. "Chairman Levy, are we for sale?" Levy replied, "Absolutely not!" He then turned to José Dedeurwaerder, his head of Renault's global sales and marketing, and said, "Isn't that correct, José?" José, his head down all the while his face turning red, said, "That's correct."

Liar, liar, French fries on fire!

On March 9, 1987, about 12 days after the AMC Board of Directors dinner in Paris, Joe Cappy received a phone call at his home at five in the morning from José Dedeurwaerder from his Paris office. José informed Cappy that Renault and Chrysler had reached an agreement whereby Chrysler would buy out Renault's interest in American Motors and tender to acquire the shares from the public. José indicated that the announcement would be made that day through a press release at noon Detroit time.

Dedeurwaerder then asked Cappy about the status of the ongoing labor discussions between AMC and Local 72 of the United Auto Workers (UAW) in Kenosha, Wisconsin. Cappy explained that AMC and Local 72 had finally reached an accord, after three tough months of talks, and planned to sign the agreement later that morning. José told Cappy to contact his people in Kenosha and tell them "under no circumstance should they sign any agreement – and that an announcement would be made at noon Detroit time that would terminate all discussions with the union."

The negotiations with Local 72 in Wisconsin revolved around reducing the number of work classifications at the Kenosha Plant to levels already in place between the UAW and the Japanese transplants in the United States – from 22 classifications to 5. There were no requests for any other concessions. In return, American Motors would commit to build a new assembly operation in Kenosha, Wisconsin, for the next ultimate Jeep vehicle: the all-new Jeep Grand Cherokee, code-named ZJ.

Before talks began with Local 72, a "heads up" breakfast meeting was held with Cappy, Dick Calmes, AMC's Vice President of Personnel and Labor Relations, and Ray Majerus, head of the UAW/AMC Group and Secretary-Treasurer of the International UAW.

The UAW's Majerus, upon hearing the proposed trade-off – a new, high-volume production vehicle in exchange for reduced worker classifications and thus plant efficiencies and cost savings – said, "This is a no brainer." However, he indicated that it had to be resolved with the leaders of Local 72, and not by him. The problem he said was a long-standing, historically poor relationship between labor and management in Kenosha. Over the years, the union was approached constantly by AMC looking for concessions, which the union accepted, without ever getting back completely what was promised in return. Majerus remarked that the Local would eventually agree with AMC's proposal, but that it will take some "soak" time.

What made matters worse was that the Local 72 was a "maverick" local with a difficult relationship with the International UAW Headquarters, primarily because the local union was an established union predating the formation of the UAW. Bottom line: the Kenosha local would not be pushed around by the UAW chieftains in Detroit.

The new facilities in Kenosha and the new product promised by AMC were going to be funded jointly from three sources: AMC, the State of Wisconsin, led by Governor Tommy Thompson, using the state's credit support as a Loan Guarantee, and Chrysler Corporation which wanted American Motors to contract-assemble some of their older, lower volume cars still in demand for which Chrysler no longer had plant capacity to build.

Off the phone and with new marching orders from José Dedeurwaerder – make that "non-marching orders" regarding the union deal – Cappy dressed and phoned his chief negotiator Dick Calmes in his motel room in Kenosha. Calmes was in Kenosha for one purpose – signing of the agreement with the UAW local. Cappy told Calmes point blank he was signing nothing. "Just stall for time" were Cappy's orders and Calmes was instructed to get on a plane back to Motown as soon as possible. Calmes started to balk, arguing how long and hard his team had been working on an agreement with the union until Cappy interrupted: "Dick, a very important announcement will be made at noon Detroit time that will clarify my instructions. Do whatever you have to, but don't sign anything."

As he drove to his office before the sun had risen, Cappy's "car phone" rang (that's what cellphones were called back then) – it was Chrysler's Ben Bidwell, one of Lee Iacocca's chief lieutenants. Bidwell told Cappy he was going to receive a hand-delivered letter in a matter of minutes and that it was urgently important. Thanks to his earlier conversation with Paris, Cappy knew what the letter would contain.

Once in his office, Cappy told his assistant Jackie Beckman to be on the lookout for someone who was to hand deliver a letter to him. Ben Bidwell had Bill O'Brien, second in command of Chrysler's Legal Staff, prepare a letter under Bidwell's signature outlining the essence of

Chrysler's purchase of American Motors from Renault and the PR release timing. Bidwell demanded that only O'Brien deliver the letter to Cappy and asked the legal beagle if he knew where AMC's HQ, the American Center, was located. O'Brien said "yes" and got in his car for the 15-minute drive from Chrysler's HQ in Highland Park to Southfield.

American Motors occupied eight of the 25 floors of the American Center. The building is positioned on 25 acres of land in the middle of "Malfunction Junction"—a confluence of the crazy-busy I-696 freeway, the Lodge Freeway from downtown Detroit to the western suburbs, and U.S. 24/Telegraph Road, one of metro Detroit's busiest boulevards. The building would be dwarfed if it was in downtown Detroit. But out in "the burbs," it stood out like an elephant on a ping pong table. In fact, it can be seen from 10 miles away in any direction. As they say, "You couldn't miss it if you tried."

Chrysler lawyer Bill O'Brien missed it. The problem for someone who was going there for the first time was determining how to get to the building itself. As the folks in New Hampshire were famous for saying, "Ya can't get there-ah from here-ah." See, you could always see it, but couldn't figure out how to get there. The next thing you knew, you were past it and when you tried to turn around you found yourself on another of the major arteries going another direction – Lansing, Flint, Toledo or Detroit.

Bill O'Brien had found himself in Detroit's version of the "Bermuda Triangle." This corporate lawyer, on the verge of becoming the top lawyer for the combined Chrysler/AMC (he got the job) had specific orders from a Chrysler honcho to get the letter to Joe Cappy as quickly as possible. But, with heavy morning traffic and not getting anywhere close anytime soon, he was about to park on the side of the highway and try to walk to the biggest building in the area he could see like the nose on his face, but could not find. It was like the scene in the movie *The Poltergeist* where Jobeth Williams is running down the hall of her house to save her little girl stolen by Satan and with every step she takes, the hallway grows in length.

O'Brien finally "exorcised" his "demons" and delivered the package to Joe Cappy. The message from Bidwell was exactly what Cappy had imagined, and he appreciated the heads-up from his former boss, friend, and soon-to-be colleague.

AMC's chief negotiator, Dick Calmes, called Joe Cappy later in a whirlwind day, hours after the announcement was made in Detroit: his message was that the UAW Local 72 members were jumping for joy that Chrysler Corporation was buying American Motors and Lee Iacocca was "saving Kenosha."

As the French would say: au contraire.

The truth was that Chrysler was not willing to make a long-term commitment regarding Kenosha. That was why

Renault's Dedeurwaerder had given Cappy the explicit instructions to not sign any labor agreement. No new assembly operations were built in Kenosha and the production of cars stopped when the automotive operations, including the big assembly plant, were closed within the next year and a half. Only the engine-building plant was left running. A workforce which could have topped 8,500 UAW workers at full capacity with car production was, as of March 2013, zero, as the last part of the Kenosha facilities met the wrecking ball.

Had an agreement between AMC and the UAW been signed earlier and the sale of AMC to Chrysler still completed, Chrysler Corporation would have been legally obligated to follow through with the new facilities and production of the all-new, groundbreaking, and mega-profitable Jeep Grand Cherokee in Kenosha, Wisconsin, instead of in a brand new mega-plant in Detroit, Michigan. The building of a new assembly plant generally guarantees production and jobs for 20 to 30 years. In the end, all of these jobs were lost due to a failure of good faith negotiations between management and union leadership, resulting from years of mistrust and difficult relationships. For Joe Cappy, the "Mayor of Wisconsin Dells," it was a sad ending in his home state.

Months later, Cappy was flying into Milwaukee and was picked up by an AMC security employee. On the drive to Kenosha, the driver told Cappy how proud he was to have worked for American Motors for the past 25 years. During that time, he had put all three of his children through college, something he never was able to achieve himself.

Cappy knew the carnage ahead for the people of Kenosha, but took some solace that a lot of good had been done.

Chapter 24
The French "Disconnection"

Joe Cappy's appointment as President and CEO of American Motors was due entirely to the efforts of his predecessor, José Dedeurwaerder – an executive Cappy greatly admired, right from the time he joined AMC.

Dedeurwaerder was a difficult man for many executives to work with, or for, but Cappy enjoyed a warm and solid relationship with him. José had a temper and was mercurial in personality. By nature, that would scare off many people. But Cappy was "seasoned" as he had worked for Paul Lorenz at Ford—a VP who would throw pencils at executives who displeased him. Lorenz was a sweetheart to those above him, but a tyrant to those working for him.

As President and CEO, Cappy continued to report to Dedeurwaerder who had returned to Renault to take over worldwide sales and marketing for the French automaker, and Joe would do anything José asked of him. So, it was a surprise when Cappy received yet another phone call from Chrysler's Ben Bidwell in mid-1987, just months after the Chrysler-Renault deal was announced, telling him that Dedeurwaerder was planning to return to American Motors to replace him. Dedeurwaerder had personally approached Lee Iacocca and asked for an Executive VP position at Chrysler and told the Chrysler CEO he was going back to AMC to replace Joe Cappy. Cappy asked Bidwell what

Iacocca thought about Dedeurwaerder's request. As usual, Bidwell was blunt: Iacocca was not interested.

While Dedeurwaerder had a strong relationship with the late Renault Chairman Georges Besse, his relationship with Besse's successor, Raymond Levy, was on the rocks. In fact, based upon reports back through Renault ex-pats in executive positions in AMC, Dedeurwaerder was going out of his way to be insubordinate to Levy, especially in front of other Renault executives.

What Dedeurwaerder didn't realize was that if he came to Joe Cappy and told him he wanted his old job back, Cappy would have gladly stepped down. Joe was comfortable he would be offered some senior position at Chrysler once the deal closed, whether he was first or second in command at AMC. But Cappy never got that courtesy. He had to hear of Dedeurwaerder's intentions from his all-too-familiar source of the truth who seemed to always be looking out for him: Ben Bidwell.

Since a call never came from Dedeurwaerder, Cappy began to think about how José would manage to get back the AMC CEO chair and concluded the only way was for José to throw him under the bus with the AMC Board of Directors. The thought incensed Cappy. He was proud of the way the company was progressing under his leadership, and didn't want his reputation ruined. Various Renault ex-pats were telling him that Dedeurwaerder was telling Renault's leaders in Paris that the new AMC plant being built in Canada and its new car under development, the Premier, were in trouble timing-wise and financially, along with engineering and component supplier problems.

An AMC Board of Directors meeting was coming up and Cappy believed was likely the time for Dedeurwaerder to bring the alleged "problems" to light, if he was going to do so. In any event, providing the Board a brief update on the plant status and car would be timely, Cappy thought.

Cappy called two of the top Renault ex-pats at AMC and José's close confidents, Jesus Peon, VP of Manufacturing, and Francois Castaing, VP of Engineering and Product; and a third VP that Dedeurwaerder lured away from General Motors, John Mowery, who was in charge of Purchasing. Cappy asked the trio to prepare presentations for the Board – an update on each of their areas of responsibility limited to 15 minutes each. He also told them to not arrive outside the boardroom until 9:15 a.m., about 45 minutes after the board meeting would begin. Their presentations would not be placed on the written meeting agenda, but needed to be ready if the time or occasion warranted.

Unknown to Cappy at the time, José Dedeurwaerder had dinner with Castaing the night before the board meeting in an attempt to "pump" Castaing about any negative comments regarding Cappy's stewardship. Despite being a fellow Renault ex-pat, Castaing didn't bite and told Dedeurwaerder that Cappy was doing a great job running the company. What's more, Castaing didn't "share" the request Cappy had made of him and his two colleagues in preparation for the next day's board meeting.

The AMC board meeting started at 8:30 a.m. and proceeded through various administrative issues. As those items wrapped up, Dedeurwaerder requested the floor: "Mr. President, I have some issues that I would like to share with the board."

The snake had landed.

Dedeurwaerder proceeded to engage the board regarding "serious issues" that had gotten back to him regarding "major problems" with the new plant, serious engineering issues with the new car, and trouble with the suppliers' readiness for the start of production. He emphasized the critical nature of the problems and the potential for failure of both the Chrysler deal (now under due diligence review) and the company as a whole.

Cappy's heart was pumping, but he remained calm. "José, I don't know who you got your information from in Paris, but it's incorrect. We are in excellent shape across the board. I was prepared to provide the Board with a brief update on our readiness if we had time, but with José's comments, I will provide an update at this time. John (board secretary), please ask the gentlemen outside to come in."

In walked the three vice presidents Cappy had earlier given assignments, anxious to tell the Board how everything they were responsible for was "on time and on budget." Cappy introduced Castaing, Peon, and Mowery and told them that the Board was concerned whether or not everything was still on track with the new plant, the new car, and the supply base.

As each of the three executives went through their 15-minute presentations, José Dedeurwaerder's head dropped lower and lower, with his face getting increasingly redder. After the three VPs finished, Cappy asked if any of the board members had questions. Zero. Nada. Utter silence, including from Dedeurwaerder. The only sound Joe Cappy could hear was from his inner voice: "Prick."

Chapter 25
Due Diligence: Hurry Up and Wait

A person might think that a due diligence review period that stretched 149 days, from March 9, 1987, to August 4, 1987, meant there were some serious issues. Actually, there was only one issue which took forever due to its "unknown" nature—Jeep CJ liability concerns.

Chrysler had been studying American Motors for two and a half years and likely knew AMC as well as the AMC management. In addition, the two companies had been exchanging information in an effort to sign a contract assembly agreement to build Chrysler's older, lower volume M and L body cars in AMC's idle Kenosha Plant. There had been meetings, plant tours, and analyses ongoing since before the fall of 1986, with an assembly agreement signed in September 1986 between the two companies.

It was interesting for Chrysler to learn the economics of Contract Assembly from AMC's view, and for AMC to learn the economics from Chrysler's view. There was plenty of incremental profit to share because the large fixed costs inherent with building all-new manufacturing capacity had already been bought and paid for.

Since Chrysler was in the same business it made things easier as well. Chrysler had spent a lot of time getting comfortable with the potential and strength of Jeep. Chrysler knew the four-wheel SUV market was going to continue to grow. And they knew the Jeep brand was known all over the world --and had American patriotism all over it because of its WWII heritage. In addition, many of the ex-Ford people who followed Lee Iacocca to Chrysler after Henry Ford II famously fired him knew Joe Cappy. And Joe knew them. So, there was an inherent level of trust, even friendship, between the parties.

The difficulty came because Chrysler would be negotiating with Renault, who would be leaving the U.S. market, but had been managing the business with its representative employees from France at the top of AMC, in concert with Joe Cappy and his management team. Chrysler would have to determine the real cost of producing the Jeep products.

Renault was also supremely cautious about revealing its financial information in the event the due diligence findings resulted in Chrysler backing out of the deal. If a suitor pulls out of a deal after due diligence, the company left at the altar is often beyond-damaged goods. In addition, since Renault was a French company with European methods of financial reporting, some of the analysis was complicated.

But those issues were merely speed bumps. The real issue to resolve, however, was how to quantify the risks and costs associated with Jeep CJ roll over litigation. It had the potential to be a pothole that could tear off the wheels of the deal.

Various models of the Jeep CJ had been manufactured since Willys Jeep had turned the World War II mechanical hero into a domestic vehicle, first for use on farms and then vehicles for the regular driving public. It was the quintessential Jeep vehicle. By the mid-1980s it was one of most common vehicles in the parking lot at Beverly Hills High School. It was "America" with all its warts.

And the Jeep CJ had more warts than a toad. While one of the greatest vehicles ever for driving "off-road," the vehicle's narrow wheelbase and relatively high center of gravity meant it had a much higher than average propensity to roll over when improperly and/or stupidly or recklessly handled. And, roll over many of them did, resulting sadly, in injuries and deaths. AMC had literally warehouses of damaged CJs inspected for litigation against the company.

The due diligence analysts from Chrysler had to review the roll over data, past litigation, current and future litigation by accident year, by calendar year, by model year, by type of accident, by type of injury, etc. They were struggling to determine if AMC had put enough reserves on its books to cover the potential liability and even more questions. Who would handle the cases? Who would settle the cases? Or fight the cases? And each side had their independent views on the potential exposure of this issue.

Both sides felt the issue of Jeep rollovers was in the rear view mirror as AMC had redesigned the vehicle in 1986, making the all-new Jeep Wrangler wider and less prone to rollover than its CJ predecessor. But, the liability potential remained in the headlights of the deal.

The CJ litigation issue was <u>the</u> key and explosive problem in reaching a fast conclusion in the due diligence review. At both companies, because litigation was so rampant by plaintiffs' bar – some warranted but much of it your basic, garden variety ambulance chasing, looking for a fast, green mail grab at money-- all of the facts and statistics gathered by the companies were kept in small, tight groups and could not be shared between the two companies.

How tight? AMC CEO Joe Cappy, was purposefully left out of CJ litigation issues and discussions to prevent him being called upon for depositions by plaintiffs' attorneys. There were only a few on the Chrysler due diligence team that were involved in these discussions as well.

Chrysler believed that Renault should be responsible for cases occurring while Renault owned the company. Chrysler would agree to be responsible for accidents and lawsuits occurring after it gained ownership of the company. In the end, the two parties agreed to divide the risks and opportunities. As it turned out, the costs were not as severe as Chrysler originally contemplated and the reserves were sufficient – in fact, in excess.

After long, drawn out reviews and discussions at Sullivan & Cromwell's NYC law offices, in a conference room appropriately nicknamed the "Fire Room," about 90 percent of the original March 1987 Memo of Understanding (MOU) was converted into detailed contract language fairly smoothly. The "Fire Room" referred to the photographs on the walls covering major fires in Manhattan, not the often fiery moments as Renault and Chrysler tried to work out the deal. The remaining 10 percent of the unresolved issues resulted in very difficult on-going negotiations.

Initially, it was unclear if the remaining unresolved issues were a genuine misunderstanding, or one party or the other trying to "re-cut" the deal to secure an advantage. All of these issues were identified and researched with the final decisions left to the chief dealmakers, Ben Bidwell and Steve Miller for Chrysler, and José Dedeurwaerder and his chief of staff, Jean-Marc Lepeu, for Renault.

A key remaining issue to deal with was the integration in Highland Park, Chrysler's headquarters, with AMC's headquarters and Tech Center. The integration of people, information systems, products, dealers, suppliers, and operations were paramount.

Smartly, Chrysler CEO Lee Iacocca gave specific direction to pick the best person for the job from either Chrysler or AMC and not to play favorites. He wanted rapid transition to one integrated company as soon as possible. Iacocca's direction was laudable, but in the real world, not likely to happen. Would you take an unknown

AMC executive over a loyal Chrysler employee that you knew? While there might be positions available for the management level below AMC's vice presidents, the AMC VPs would be at high risk to find a comparable position at Chrysler.

Because of that, Dick Calmes, VP Personnel and Labor Relations, and Joe Cappy put together, with AMC's law firm Jones Day, severance agreements for the 14 AMC executive officers. When Chrysler learned of the plan, Cappy received a call from Steve Miller telling him that he was jeopardizing the entire deal. Miller claimed it was a gigantic mistake and that Cappy needed to cancel the plan. If not, Miller predicted the failure of the entire deal and that it would all be on Cappy's head.

Joe Cappy was in a hell of a pickle, but channeled Muhammad Ali and pulled a "rope-a-dope" routine and let Miller punch himself out. Cappy knew that if the roles were reversed, Miller would most likely install this type of plan for his fellow comrades. As expected, the AMC outside independent directors agreed with the severance plan agreements and they were put in place. Chrysler did not protest.

Lee Iacocca scheduled a meeting at the Bloomfield Hills Country Club with his executive committee, where first Joe Cappy provided his evaluation of his direct reports. Following Joe, each AMC Vice President individually was invited in to meet and talk with the top team. In this manner, each AMC executive had the opportunity to sell themselves to Chrysler.

As it turned out, Chrysler offered three AMC officers comparable positions at Chrysler: Joe Cappy, CFO John Tierney, and Product VP Francois Castaing. Of the remaining 13 officers, excluding José Dedeurwaerder and Pierre Semerena, eight resigned under the AMC severance plan, and five took lesser positions at Chrysler. Chrysler wanted to hire Cappy's PR chief, Jerry Sloan, for a comparable PR slot and made him a very attractive offer, but Sloan elected to return to the Ford Motor Company where he would eventually retire from to become a college professor.

Overall Chrysler offered positions to some 100 of the top 125 AMC executives – high performance/potential P-Roll Executives, the level just below vice president at AMC. All of them performed exceptionally well at Chrysler. Since Chrysler didn't have any legitimate overseas/international business, AMC's International staff almost got picked up entirely. And, the AMC people soared within Chrysler. Why? Former Chrysler President Jim Holden put it best: "AMC people were more broadly experienced on average, as compared with their Chrysler counterparts. This was based upon the AMC culture of working with more limited resources where they were more resourceful, more creative, and more able to cut bureaucratic corners to get things done cheaper, faster, and often times better. The AMC people were used to wearing multiple hats and getting more things done quickly, and it was noticeable."

More than 70 percent of AMC's salaried work force weathered the merger and were offered and accepted jobs at Chrysler. Cappy had expected 50 percent at best, and for him it was a very positive sign that Chrysler was being fair and impartial in the selection process.

Next to acquiring the Jeep brand, in importance, was Chrysler's decision to import the entire Jeep Engineering Operation, lock, stock, and barrel. Francois Castaing, AMC's Group VP, Product and Quality, had put into place at AMC a "platform team approach" for Jeep. Both Lee Iacocca and Chrysler co-Chairman and product guru Bob Lutz realized that this new approach to product development, which the Japanese were using so effectively, was the "wedge" Chrysler needed to replace its old, functional silo organization so entrenched at Chrysler. In the Chrysler of "old," designers fought with engineers, engineers fought with the manufacturing folks and everybody hated sales and marketing.

The platform-team type of organization improved timing to development and production, decreased manufacturing time, increased efficiency, improved quality, and lowered manufacturing costs. It eliminated waste and inefficiency and the redo of product by all of the functional groups. Its positive effect on Chrysler over the next five years would be breathtaking.

Gerald Greenwald, Chrysler Motors Chairman, asked Joe Cappy to be the lead integrator for the two companies. To accomplish this task, Cappy and AMC needed to lay out 100 percent of the functions of each AMC section and department, line by line. Then it was necessary to discover where each of those functions would go into Chrysler, and have the Chrysler recipient accept the responsibility. This was a major task. One single AMC department, for example, went into 28 different Chrysler areas. This was not necessarily a shot at Chrysler, as had General Motors acquired AMC, the single department would most likely go into 100 different areas at the behemoth company.

By March 1, 1988, only seven months into the merger, 13 of the 19 functional areas were 100-percent integrated, and four of the remaining six were at 95 percent or better. By today's standard, it was breathtaking. The systems integration was the largest hurdle to complete, and would take almost two years to finalize.

After the announcement of the Chrysler/Renault agreement on March 9, 1987, Joe Cappy realized that as CEO of American Motors, he had the responsibility to continue to run the company, ensure that all AMC employees maintained their duties without exception, achieve their objectives, and remain comfortable in their positions, despite the severe uncertainty they all faced regarding their jobs and the fate of their families.

In order to fulfill their mission, AMC needed to have full transparency and discipline throughout the company. To accomplish the teamwork necessary, Cappy established Monday and Friday meetings with all officers on hand, where all of the contacts between Chrysler and AMC employees took place during the due diligence period were reviewed and discussed to keep everyone fully informed. This group was keenly aware that until the due diligence portion of the sale process was completed, Chrysler could decide not to proceed with the acquisition and AMC would be a stand-alone company again (and this time, possibly without Renault support), but then with a tarnished reputation.

The process worked exceptionally well. Everyone was informed and felt part of the process. The exchange of information allowed unresolved issues to be addressed and corrected by executives in all areas of the company. Minutes of these meetings were kept by Cappy's Assistant, Jackie Beckman, and distributed extensively throughout the company.

AMC was not going to be criticized or held responsible for letting projects/programs be delayed or letting the organization fall apart.

But sadly, not everyone in the AMC family fared well, thanks mainly to a double cross in Cappy's home state of Wisconsin that would turn ugly.

Chapter 26
The Wisconsin Multi-Double Cross

"Eight times in five years is too many." –Ed Stegall, UAW Local 72, Kenosha, Wisconsin.

That comment from a United Auto Workers (UAW) Local 72 officer is a slight exaggeration, but fairly close to the truth. It reflects the frustration arising when a company is losing money, yet having to invest huge amounts of capital to remain competitive, continues to reach out to all areas of the company to cut costs and puts a bullseye on labor costs.

In an automotive industry where the organized labor, like the UAW, was accommodating foreign auto manufacturers with special concessions to build assembly plants in the United States, many of the domestic manufacturers found themselves at a significant disadvantage regarding the cost of labor.

As always, the best plans go awry with changes in management, gasoline prices, consumer behavior, economic conditions, product appeal, complexity of operation, and industry demand. As conditions change, the smaller, weaker companies need to react quickly to stay competitive. This, of course, is the opposite of what the labor force prefers. Ergo, conflict arises.

American Motors had both – it was smaller and weaker than its competitors and it had conflict with labor up the ying-yang.

The major problems with UAW Local 72 and the State of Wisconsin started in November 1981, when AMC proposed an investment by the workers that would be repaid in 1984. Local 72 was asked to consider an investment in the company of 10 percent of the wages and benefits from its members working for AMC – about $115 million. This investment would earn 10 percent interest, compounded annually, and be repaid in 1984. The union agreed in April 1982.

As 1984 came around, the repayment was delayed until 1985, and now in the form of profit sharing, or a "wheel tax" of $100 per vehicle produced in North America for four years beginning in 1985. The "wheel tax" would provide each worker around $2,800 per year for each of the next four years.

One year later, AMC indicated that they were short of cash and would have to defer repayment until conditions improved, and they needed to talk about further concessions from the union immediately. In mid-July 1985 after many discussions and the company threatening the closing of the Milwaukee and Kenosha plants by mid-1986, if not earlier, the two UAW locals (72 and 75) agreed to a wage rollback of $.37 cents per hour, the loss of 40 hours of paid vacation and nine paid days off. This agreement was to run through August 1988.

Shortly thereafter, AMC and Chrysler entered discussions to have AMC perform contract assembly for Chrysler, using the under-utilized AMC Kenosha plant. The plan was for AMC to assemble Chrysler's older full-sized rear-wheel-drive M-body cars: Chrysler 5th Avenue, Dodge Diplomat, and Plymouth Gran Fury. As part of this agreement, the State of Wisconsin would provide more than $3 million to help train 2,700 AMC workers to assemble the Chrysler products.

As talks dragged on, the complexities increased. Talks now included contract assembly for Chrysler's old L-body small cars as well: the Dodge Omni and Plymouth Horizon. AMC now wanted increased concessions from the State, as well as the UAW. To mix it up even more, AMC tossed a new Jeep product into the mix with the goal of building new facilities for a body shop and a paint shop, plus renovations for the main assembly facility.

In January 1987, Wisconsin Governor Tommy G. Thompson, a Republican, intervened. Faith and coincidence, and promises, showed up again. Governor Thompson was from Elroy, Wisconsin, a small town northwest of Wisconsin Dells where Joe Cappy went to high school. Governor Thompson remarked that when you hail from Elroy, Wisconsin, you have to be an optimist just to get up in the morning.

One of Cappy's teammates on the Dells' 1952 championship high school football team was Jim Wimmer, now a successful lobbyist headquartered in Madison, Wisconsin. Wimmer, a staunch Democrat, had two notches on his six gun – one was being the successful campaign manager for former Democratic Governor Patrick Lucey, who had been Wisconsin's chief negotiator with AMC since October 1985, and the second being he was the fellow who talked Joe Cappy into joining the Young Democrat's Club when Cappy was 16 years old.

Governor Thompson had a private dinner at the Governor's Mansion for Cappy and his high school pal to discuss the project and the obstacles facing approval of the financial support from the state AMC sought. Wimmer believed that the Democrats would eventually get behind the effort.

Governor Thompson threw himself behind AMC's campaign to win state financial assistance and to get the additional concessions needed from the UAW in Kenosha to bring more jobs to the state and secure the jobs already in place. In summary, AMC and Chrysler would pay $400 million, with the State of Wisconsin contributing through loan guarantees worth $200 million, and with Local 72 agreeing to pay cuts of 15 percent that would be restored gradually over the life of the contract (42 months). It was yet another "pinky swear" moment.

Then, without warning, the Chrysler/Renault announcement hit and everything was off the table. But, there was joy in Mudville. Freddie Kuzrich's bar across the street from the Kenosha plant's Gate 15 immediately put on its billboard sign, "Iacocca for President." A Jeep worker in Toledo, Cliff Shively, commented: "Whatever (Iacocca) touches turns to gold – it's just like Christ coming back."

The euphoria in Toledo and Kenosha among the rank and file continued all through the spring and summer of 1987 as its "savior," Chrysler, performed its due diligence of the potential hook-up with AMC.

Once Chrysler's acquisition of AMC was complete on August 5, 1987, a monkey wrench was almost immediately thrown into the works as the U.S. economy started to tank, taking the automotive industry with it. Less than three months after the acquisition was complete, America (and the world) was hit with Black Monday. On October 19, 1987, the Dow Jones Industrial Average lost 22.6 percent of its value in one day, dropping 508 points to 1,738.74.

Faster than Wall Street executives could jump out the window and splat on the sidewalk, the demand and need for old M-body and L-body Chrysler cars went kaput, as did the need for contract assembly work with AMC and its union employees. Chrysler first laid-off one shift in Kenosha days after Black Monday, and in January 1988, Chrysler announced it would close the Kenosha Assembly plant, permanently terminating 5,500 workers. The obsolete Kenosha Plant and its people were, in a word, expendable.

Governor Thompson, state politicians, local Kenosha officials, and the UAW, were outraged and accused Chrysler of breaking its promise to keep the plant open for five years. Rudy Kuzel, leader of Local 72, supported by the UAW International Headquarters, promised to "make the plant closing the most expensive in history if Chrysler did not reconsider."

Local 72 rented a billboard and posted the message, "Iacocca, keep your word to Kenosha." Freddie's Bar billboard, which just months before urged "Iacocca for President," replaced those words with "Iacocca is a whore."

Rudy Kuzel wasn't going to sit around and wait for Chrysler to think it over. He went into attack mode. He talked to everyone he could in an effort to keep the heat on Chrysler. He planned a major rally for all of Local 72 members and other interested Kenosha citizens, and invited outside speakers from the UAW International and union supporters to talk at a rally in front of the plant on 52nd Avenue in Kenosha.

Kuzel was speaking to his team as if they were behind by two touchdowns. But, he was a football coach somewhat out of his mind. He was rocking and rolling as he was introducing his main speaker: "When you are up against this kind of opposition and power in Chrysler, you need all of strength you can muster. You need firepower, and we have it with us tonight!! I'm proud to introduce one of the strongest spear-chuckers in this country: the Reverend Jesse Jackson!"

That's right, the local UAW president had just called one of the visible African-Americans in the United States, the head of the Rainbow Coalition, a "spear chucker."

Jackson gave Kuzel a startled look but dutifully carried on his duty of whipping up the crowd against Chrysler.

As the days went on, Rudy Kuzel outlined the carnage the Kenosha Plant carried. As of July 1, 1984, AMC's Kenosha operations employed 2,500 people, with another 6,500 employees on layoff. He added to that about 12,500 retirees. Chrysler's abandonment of the Wisconsin city would, according to the union leader, impact a total of 21,500 men and woman, plus their families. All told: about 45,000 people

On February 16, 1988, Lee Iacocca held a press conference in Milwaukee, Wisconsin, to announce Chrysler's response to help the families of Kenosha autoworkers who were losing their jobs due to the plant closing. Iacocca announced a $20 million trust fund to aid unemployed former-AMC-now-Chrysler plant workers. The local union leaders called the gesture inadequate.

Chrysler had already announced that it would extend the Omni/Horizon production until January 1989. In May 1988, Chrysler agreed to repay the workers most of the more than one hundred million dollars in concessions that they had been granted earlier to American Motors. Each worker would get a lump sum ranging from $5,000 to $10,000. Chrysler also funded the bankrupt AMC SUB Fund providing 24 weeks of Supplemental Unemployment Benefits.

In the end, the payments to former AMC hourly employees, who were for such a short time new Chrysler employees, cost Chrysler Corporation a little more than $100 million.

In September 1988, Chrysler offered the City of Kenosha an aid package valued at $200 million under the condition that Kenosha would not sue Chrysler. Kenosha had no choice and accepted Chrysler's offer.

The Wisconsin Multi-Double Cross was history.

Chapter 27
Will the Eagle Fly?

Once Chrysler understood, and accepted, that in order to acquire the Jeep brand they would have to purchase all of American Motors – warts and all – they also knew they would have to provide a line-up of car products to sell alongside Jeep vehicles.

The AMC dealer network was somewhat of a "dog's breakfast." Due to state franchise laws, the AMC network was comprised of three separate dealership networks: some dealers were American Motors dealers, some just Jeep vehicle dealers, and then some just Renault dealers. Or, a combination of all two or three. It was the definition of what the U.S. Marines call a cluster-f--k, or a FUBAR.

But, it wasn't all that bad compared to Chrysler's own dealer network. The AMC network was selling the sub-compact Renault Alliance and Encore hatchback, the most modern, up-to-date car products in their line-up. Combined with two new Jeep products, the Jeep Cherokee and Jeep Wagoneer, the AMC dealers were actually selling more vehicles per outlet than the Chrysler networks by a factor of ten percent.

With Renault and its vehicles out of the picture, Chrysler would have to create a new and competitive passenger car brand to take advantage of the dealer body it would inherit and to encourage Jeep dealers to reduce their dependence on competitive passenger car/truck products from General Motors, Ford, and the Japanese brands.

But, Chrysler management was in a pickle: they didn't want to upset the existing Chrysler, Plymouth, and Dodge car and truck dealers after the acquisition of American Motors. After all, these dealerships, mostly family-owned small businesses, stood by Chrysler years earlier as it had danced near bankruptcy. Chrysler's core dealership owners would see their new family member from American Motors competing for attention, corporate investment funds, and critical marketing dollars like advertising and rebates.

At the same time Chrysler officials considered and then quickly discarded as unacceptable the "badge engineering" of any Chrysler, Plymouth, or Dodge vehicle for the American Motors dealer network.

Chrysler wanted to go slowly until they really understood the AMC dealers they were inheriting. And what would be the family of products sitting in the dealerships alongside venerable and hugely profitable Jeep vehicles? What would the brand be named and how would it be targeted?

Selling high-end cars in the new American Motors dealer network did not seem appropriate, despite the fact that tons of Jeep buyers were, in fact, high-end consumers who more often than not bought their Jeeps with cash in their wallets. Their "demographics" were off the charts. People buying Jeep vehicles, had a Benz or a BMW, as their everyday driver. But putting a new, developed luxury brand in the AMC dealerships would totally piss off a Chrysler dealer network that had been abused, screwed, and tattooed over the past decade. And, worse yet, more mid-priced cars would be direct competitors to Chrysler's existing Plymouth and Dodge brands.

Chrysler was in a quandary. Offering low-priced cars to the new network, mostly Jeep dealers, would bring low profits and probably not get them to relinquish their other non-Chrysler branded cars—including Mercedes Benz, BMW and the like. Worse yet, providing the new network with Chrysler, Plymouth, or Dodge products would, in most cases, violate dealer agreements where distance between dealership locations was too close. Market research on these issues failed to provide any viable solution.

Frustrated, Chrysler CEO Lee Iacocca and Ben Bidwell, Executive VP of Sales and Marketing, decided that recreating the Eagle brand was the best path forward. American Motors had unsuccessfully used Eagle as its brand for its four-wheel-drive passenger car products. Still, Iacocca and Bidwell thought re-creating the Eagle brand would give the former AMC dealers a car line to stand alongside the fabulous Jeep vehicles.

There was little, if any, "push-back" against the proposal. Seriously, who would want to debate the two most successful marketing people in the automotive industry and the most famous CEO in the history of business? Nobody, baby!

And so it was. A new brand was born: Eagle, same name as the snack company providing patrons a small pack of peanuts on the airplane. There was Eagle-brand condensed milk. Eagle, Eagle, Eagle was everywhere. Worse yet, AMC had started an Eagle brand of four-wheel-drive passenger cars that bombed in the marketplace. WTF?

The answer to the question of, "Will the Eagle fly?" is that there weren't enough fish in the Detroit River to feed on, so the Eagle motored out of Motown. Actually, the die was cast well before Chrysler's acquisition, with the selection of the first "Eagle" car's styling.

Before the acquisition of AMC, Renault's José Dedeurwaerder, the one-time head of American Motors, engaged three independent design chiefs and studios to develop styling properties based upon the vehicle's specifications. All three completed styling models were market-researched. The styling property selected was the one with the highest overall average score. It was a handsome property, designed by Giorgetto Giugiaro of Italdesign. Giugiaro had styled more than 200 vehicles on his resume. He was a master among masters. Due to his European background, the car he designed for what would become Chrysler's fledgling Eagle brand was quite similar in appearance to an Audi already on the market. So, with the highest "average" market research score and its European look, it was a very conservative and safe choice.

If Chrysler Vice-Chairman and product guru Bob Lutz had been there as part of the selection process, he most assuredly would not have chosen the Giugiaro model. Lutz believed that what you should concentrate on is the styling model that has the greatest number of "nines and tens" scores – the passionate people that absolutely love the style and will do anything to buy it – even if that model has the most "ones and twos." Lutz believed "polarization" was the key to developing a breakout product and Chrysler would prove Lutz's vision correct in the coming years with the Ram pickup, PT Cruiser, and Dodge Viper. After all, why build a look-alike Audi when the real thing had already established itself as a winner in the marketplace?

One of the rejected styling models did receive polarizing "ones" and "twos" and "nines" and "tens." Its design was quite unique, but with money for just one bet at the gaming table, it was difficult to make the call for fear it would be later criticized for a styling theme that was too far-out from its competitors. Caution was the code word as a number of previous French "avant-garde" cars looked "odd" compared to their competition and bombed outside of the French marketplace. So, the "safe" Eagle Premier entered the marketplace with one tire tied behind its back.

Launching the Eagle brand became an awkward event, since the only car that the now-Jeep/Eagle dealers would have initially was the carry-over Renault Alliance and Encore models, which would be re-badged as the Eagle Alliance, a misfit in name and product attributes for the vision of Eagle. You just don't start an all-new brand with old, rotting produce with an already tarnished image of lousy quality.

After some debate, Chrysler's engineering team determined that due to some concerns over the new Premier's transmission and electrical components, the launch of the Eagle Premier, planned for the fall of 1987, would be delayed until the following spring.

So when the annual Dealer Announcement Show was held in Las Vegas, the Eagle team created a "Promise for the Future" for the AMC dealer network in attendance. Some 3,000 dealers, general managers, wives, and mistresses also known as "nieces" found a full-size, real, live Eagle flying over their head in the convention center. A review of the Eagle Premier, along with test-drives and technical seminars were held and hints of future Eagle products to come were presented.

An Eagle Premier Dealer Introduction Show was then held in Detroit with figure skating star Dorothy Hamill and her "ice review" at the home arena for the Detroit Red Wings with great success and fanfare. Lee Iacocca loved the show, but the Eagle Premier had too much on its back to fly. To launch the new brand to the public, a television commercial was shown during Super Bowl XXII where the

Washington Redskins smoked the Denver Broncos. But without strong follow-up marketing funds behind that ad, the Eagle looked more like a dead duck.

The Renault Alliance launch had received a significant boost after its launch by winning *Motor Trend* magazine's "Car of the Year." No such luck for the Eagle Premier. The only thing that the Premier received was "friendly fire" when Chrysler decided to also throw a Dodge Monaco badge on the Premier – a self-inflicted, brand-killing maneuver which unfortunately was a common practice at Chrysler for years. Chrysler had earlier pledged never to pimp its existing brands in order to help the newly-formed Eagle brand. But, they had no problem pimping Eagle. The former AMC dealer body, now Jeep/Eagle dealers, quickly turned their back on the Premier as they could not compete with the more powerful, larger, and better capitalized Dodge dealer body.

On top of that, various quality issues continued to hang around to further slowdown sales. Ralph Sarotte, General Manager of the Eagle Brand, reporting to the new head of the Jeep/Eagle brands, Joe Cappy, personally experienced the irony and futility of the quality effort. Sarotte took a family road trip out east and experienced four separate instances where the Premier would not restart after it was turned off, until the entire electrical system was allowed to cool off for a couple of hours. Twice he had the car towed to a dealership for testing and analysis and no "problem" could be found to correct – merely ghosts in the machine. It was the Renault Fuego all over again. The former AMC, now Chrysler executive Cappy, had already seen that horror movie.

As the Eagle Premier continued to suffer in the market, Chrysler was discussing possible car products for the Jeep/Eagle dealers with car companies around the world, with the best possibilities coming from Japan's Mitsubishi and Korea's Hyundai. Chrysler failed to come to any agreement with Hyundai. Before the talks broke down, a friend of Joe Cappy sent him a glass model of a Hyundai sedan with a broken wheel and a note: "This represents Hyundai quality." Not true of course, but everyone had something to say, especially if it was negative.

Chrysler did acquire an attractive 2+2 affordable sports car sourced by Mitsubishi out of its Bloomington/Normal, Illinois, plant where it was beginning production of the Mitsubishi Eclipse. The car was named the Eagle Talon, available in front-wheel and all-wheel-drive. The Talon was phenomenal and was launched in the media by Joe Cappy's new PR guy, Jason Vines, whom Cappy was grooming to be an Eagle marketing executive before the Eagle PR guy was abruptly fired. The Friday before the Monday Vines was to join Cappy's marketing team, he received a call from Steve Harris, the former AMC PR executive who had been given the number two PR position at Chrysler. "Hey Jason, Joe Cappy wants you to take the open Eagle PR spot instead of marketing." Vines didn't initially know what to say until he blurted out, "PR, Marketing? What's the difference?" "Don't worry," Harris continued, "Joe loves you."

The development of the Eagle Talon also showed that when a company has an iconic and legendary leader, it can sometimes be costly and unproductive. Eagle executives and Chrysler's design staff had gathered in the "design dome" to view an early prototype of the new sports car. It would be Chrysler CEO Lee Iacocca's first chance to see it. His initial reaction? "It was horsey." The other executives were puzzled, but immediately ordered the vehicle back to the studio for a new design. Weeks later, after spending hundreds of thousands of dollars re-designing the Talon, Iacocca was given a fresh look.

"What happened to the original design," Iacocca asked. Iacocca was then reminded of his earlier "horsey" comment. "I liked it. It reminded me of the original (Ford) Mustang." No one had had the balls to ask Iacocca what he meant by his original comments. Chrysler returned to the original design.

The Talon turned out to be a great car, but it was too little, too late. Chrysler could not afford to deliver sufficient car product or marketing support over the long haul for another brand, in addition to Jeep, Chrysler, Plymouth, and Dodge car and truck. The Eagle brand was abandoned after only a little more than three years and then began a further consolidation of all of the Chrysler Corporation dealer networks, especially when the Plymouth brand was dropped.

Lee Iacocca, the man who personally led the campaign to restore the aging Statue of Liberty, had his decades-long dream of launching a brand with the ultimate American name, Eagle, dashed. Ironically, while fixing France's gift to the United States as a sign of friendship, Iacocca and his team had failed to fix a turkey of a gift from France's Renault. Gobble, gobble and good bye, Eagle.

Chapter 28
Jeep, the Unsung Hero, Sings

The Jeep brand was misnamed: it should be called the "Jesus" brand, as it was and is a savior for its multiple owners over the last 75 years. A common thread of success in the history of Willys, Kaiser, American Motors, Chrysler, and now Fiat, is the iconic Jeep brand.

And maybe, literally, in helping save the world.

Wow! Heavy lift? Not really. During World War II, the original Jeep military vehicle became so valuable for the Allied forces that the U.S. Government ordered Willys (Jeep's "creator": Honestly, Willys stole the design from a small Pennsylvania manufacturer called Bantam and Chrysler, upon acquiring Jeep almost 50 years later, admitted as much) to give the "Jeep" design to the much bigger Ford Motor Company to also make the vehicle to support the fight against the Nazis and the Japanese aggressors. Ironically, Ford Motor Company actually made a few thousand more Jeep vehicles for the war than Willys did.

Think about it: imagine the U.S. Government saying we need more i-Pads and giving Apple's technology to Samsung to build more i-Pads. But, it was the war-of-wars, the second one, and perhaps in the case of building Jeep vehicles, the future of humanity was on the line, not access to the Internet. Geez.

During World War II, Willys and the Ford Motor Company filled more than 600,000 U.S. Government orders for Jeep vehicles. Tiny Bantam supplied only about 2,700 Jeep vehicles, with most given to America's allies, Great Britain and the Soviet Union. Yep, that Soviet Union.

And how did the Jeeps handle their load for the Allies against The Axis of Germany, Japan, and Italy? The late General George C. Marshall, the man who later spearheaded the U.S.-led rebuilding of war-torn Europe with "The Marshall Plan," called the Jeep vehicle, "America's greatest contribution to modern warfare."

Jeep's impact was clear and present, while in danger. The Jeep vehicles served in every World War II Theater as a litter bearer, machine gun firing mount, reconnaissance vehicle, pickup truck, front line limousine, ammo-bearer, wire-layer, and taxi.

In the Ardennes during the 1944-45 Battle of the Bulge – perhaps the most horrific in modern military history – Jeep vehicles loaded with stretchers and draped with wounded Allied soldiers, raced to safety ahead of spearheading Nazi armor.

In the sands of the Sahara, the morass of New Guinea, and the snow fields of Iceland, Jeep vehicles hauled the .37mm anti-tank cannons to firing sites. In Egypt, the British used a combat patrol version of Jeep vehicles to knock out a fleet of Nazi fuel tankers en route to Field Marshall Rommel's armed forces on the eve of the Battle of El Alamein. In the Pacific Theater at Guadalcanal, one of the most intense battles in military history, Jeep vehicles went in with the U.S. Marines.

This unique line of vehicles that first served so nobly in WWII, transitioned successfully to commercial success also salvaged all of the aforementioned companies which owned it. Given proper management attention and nurtured with resources, Jeep products have saved many companies with its return on investment.

When World War II ended, Willys-Overland, Jeep's owner, held true to its war production motto: "The sun never sets on the Willys-Built Jeep," by creating a civilian role for its famed Jeep vehicles.

Most important, Jeep vehicles just kept going. After an abnormal ten years of ownership – the leader by far in the industry – Jeeps were often sold to second and third buyers to use on off-road trails and as hunting vehicles. And, sometimes to people that, hell, "just wanted to finally own a Jeep."

Years later, with all sorts of Jeep vehicles in the hands of regular American drivers, Jeep's marketing tagline, "Only in a Jeep," should have, historically, been recast as "Only because of Jeep."

When Chrysler CEO Lee Iacocca was asked why he wanted to buy American Motors he responded, "Jeep is the best known automotive brand name in the world" and, at the time, only the Coke brand had higher recognition than Jeep throughout the world.

After WWII, Kaiser Industries decided to enter the automotive business that was booming with consumers and returning servicemen starved for new vehicles. It looked like "easy pickings" to the successful shipbuilding industrialist Henry Kaiser, who teamed with an automotive executive, Joseph Frazer, to manufacture Kaiser-Frazer passenger cars until 1955 when the company subsequently found the capital requirements and the stiff competition too difficult to continue producing in the United States, it moved its operations to South America.

But, two years earlier in 1953, Kaiser purchased Willys-Overland, manufacturer of the Jeep line of utility vehicles for $60 million and changed its name to first, Willys Motors, and then ten years later to Kaiser-Jeep.

After American Motors' Chairman Roy Chapin, Jr. purchased Jeep in 1970, the company's passenger car production and sales remained fairly constant, while Jeep production and sales continued to increase. By 1978, Jeep production was almost 42 percent of AMC's total production. Jeep sales kept AMC afloat through the end of Roy Chapin, Jr.'s leadership in 1978 and proved to be his most important action for the profitability and survival of the company.

At the time "the French Connection" started between AMC and Renault, the classic Jeep products were a small

CJ-5 and longer wheel base CJ-7, as well as the U.S. Postal
Service unit DJ-5, all being direct descendants of the WWII
military vehicles. They were not upscale in content, nor
owned by upscale owners. Also in the line-up was the
much larger Jeep Grand Wagoneer (and Jeep Cherokee –
codenamed SJ) that had more car-like features, comfort,
and safety.

How revered was Jeep? Enzo Ferrari said, "Jeep is
America's only real sports car." It was a shot and a huge
compliment.

During the initial talks with Renault, American Motors
was careful to keep its work on the next generation Jeep
products secret, including the soon-to-be-released XJ line-
up of mid-sized two- and four-door Jeep vehicles,
introduced as the Jeep Cherokee. And as Renault proceeded
to increase its stake in AMC to advance its Renault-based
and sourced passenger cars, the French finally got their
grips around the new Jeep vehicles under development.

Renault officials were "very pleasantly surprised" with
the new Jeep products, which promised more car-like
features, similar to the auto industry's pick-up trucks that
were loading their trucks with car features, options, and
comfort. The new XJ product – Jeep Cherokee – was
planned to hit the market in late 1983.

The XJ design concept was to preserve the Jeep DNA
(true four-wheel drive) with passenger car handling and
comfort. Since the XJ would not be derived from a truck

chassis, it would be possible to use a uni-body (passenger car) structure and a front suspension and rear suspension that combined off-road capability with excellent ride and handling on regular roads and highways.

"Market studies indicate that more than half of the sales of 4WD vehicles by 1985 will be in the compact segment, compared with only two percent in 1978," said then-Marketing Group VP Joe Cappy in the fall of 1983. With those words, Jeep introduced the 1984 XJ, the Jeep Cherokee two-door and four-door models and four-door Wagoneer sport-wagons. The $250 million AMC investment proved to be wise. The XJs, particularly the Jeep Cherokee, were more than overnight success stories as they became the only sport utility vehicle to be named "4x4 of the Year" by the three major off-road magazines. Cappy had luckily underbid his showcase: By 1985, more than 70 percent of 4WD vehicle sales were in the compact segment, basically created by Jeep.

The XJ would be available in both two-door and four-door versions, but the four-door would be the star as Ford and Chevrolet sold only two-door versions of its mid-size SUVs. Losers!

Introduced as the Jeep Cherokee and Jeep Wagoneer, the older and larger SJ Jeep Cherokee was dropped and the only larger Jeep would be the faux wood-sided Jeep Grand Wagoneer, a unique vehicle with horrible quality but with an owner base, now known as the "One-Percenters," who paid cash for the vehicle more often than not, and loved the vehicle and its "quirkiness."

The fact is the Jeep Cherokee (and its sibling Wagoneer) literally introduced the public to a new SUV segment of the industry that would grow rapidly then explode in the early 1990s thanks to Jeep (with its Grand Cherokee) and Ford Motor Company with its Ford Explorer. Billions would be made.

Scrolling back to 1986 when Chrysler was considering the purchase of American Motors, Lee Iacocca's company didn't have an entry in the growing segment, where its market size had more than quadrupled, growing from 147,000 vehicles in 1981 to 817,000 in 1986. It was a gaping hole in the Chrysler product lineup.

Iacocca saw that the new Jeep products were a smash hit with the public, appealing to cross-over passenger car customers – especially women who valued the safety and versatility of four-wheel drive and a higher driver's position for improved highway visibility and the convenience of four doors.

As Chrysler continued the art of the deal, the Jeep engineers, led by Castaing, Craig Winn, Chris Theodore, planner Jim Julow, and designers Vince Geracy and Bob Nixon, were working on a slightly larger and sleeker version of the XJ line, code-named ZJ. At first, the ZJ was to replace the XJ products, but as time passed it was certain that both products could thrive in the marketplace at different price points.

The Chrysler purchase of American Motors complete, Joe Cappy was soon put in charge of the Jeep/Eagle Division, along with his assignment to integrate American Motors into the Chrysler family. Chrysler was now faced with another bird to feed in its nest – sorely without enough resources to spread evenly.

The Dodge Division desperately wanted an SUV product in its lineup as the market was starting to explode with a rumored new breakthrough product from Ford Motor Company. But there wasn't enough capital available at Chrysler to allow Jeep to launch its all-new ZJ and build an SUV for the bigger, badder Dodge Division. So, what to do?

Chrysler CEO Lee Iacocca decided to stage a gunfight at the OK Corral. He requested both divisions – Dodge and Jeep – to prepare position papers. Joe Cappy, reporting to Ben Bidwell, would make the case for Jeep, while Ron Boltz, an incredibly bright product planner and Vice President reporting to Chrysler Vice-Chairman and product wunderkind Bob Lutz, would prepare the paper for Dodge. Cappy and his team, headed by Jim Julow put together the Jeep paper and had it blessed by Bidwell. Boltz and his team did the same for Dodge with Lutz's blessing.

Then, two wrinkles: Joe Cappy and Ron Boltz would present their positions to Iacocca and his Executive

Committee in person and Iacocca announced a change in reporting at the top of the company that resulted in Cappy now reporting to Lutz.

Cappy asked Bidwell if he should change anything in his paper due to the change in the reporting relationship. "Present as is," was Bidwell's advice.

The competing pleas from both Jeep and Dodge to get the all-new SUV were made in front of Chrysler's top brass. Exhausted, Joe Cappy returned to his office across the parking lot of Chrysler's headquarters' campus in one of the most crime-ridden sections of Detroit. Although he was now a "Chrysler Man," he hoped he had been persuasive for the home team, Jeep.

Minutes later, Bob Lutz was on the phone. "Congratulations, Joe, the ZJ will be a Jeep. But, hear me out, in the future we will never again present before the Chairman without complete agreement in advance."

Cappy fully understood the admonition, telling Lutz, "Yes, sir."

The ZJ product, branded the Jeep Grand Cherokee, was and remains one of the biggest successes in the history of the auto industry; hell, business. After its initial launch into the marketplace, there was a major slowdown in the global economy and automotive industry. But the Jeep Grand Cherokee crossed the Rubicon, and along with the other Jeep vehicles produced $2 billion in profits, which, coupled with the same profit from Chrysler's minivan sales made up for the company's other products and activities that lost $4 billion.

The American Motors acquisition by Chrysler was the single most ingenious move the legendary CEO Lee Iacocca made. And it is clear that Renault made a monumental mistake by rushing to sell AMC to Chrysler just at the time when AMC was starting to have a major, strong, and sustained turnaround with its powerful Jeep line-up.

The Jeep brand went on to save Chrysler from bankruptcy more than once and continues today to be a huge and ever-increasing success for Fiat-Chrysler on a global basis. Help save a world yesterday; save a new company today?

Just a few years into being the new steward of the Jeep brand and on the 50th anniversary of Jeep's birth, Chrysler CEO Lee Iacocca summed it up best:

"A little more than three years ago a legend was entrusted to me and the people of Chrysler Corporation. That legend is Jeep.

"As it has for half a century, the Jeep name evokes images of freedom. Jeep vehicles have always given us the distinctly American freedom to go where we want, when we want.

"The Jeep brand traces its roots to World War II, where a four-wheel-drive utility vehicle developed by Willys-Overland distinguished itself the world over. It became such a lasting symbol of our country that in 1964 a Willys-built Jeep MB was accepted for permanent display by the Smithsonian Institute in Washington, D.C.

"Along the way, Jeep vehicles have become an American icon, an indelible part of our heritage.

"The engineers and designers that turned the Jeep vehicle from a military weapon into the world's first civilian utility vehicle would probably be amazed at today's phenomenal sport utility market. Over the past fifty years, those people transformed Jeep from a vehicle of military necessity to the ultimate fun machine."

Iacocca's words, a quarter century ago, stand tall today. And now, in 2016, Jeep celebrates its 75th anniversary. Italian automaker Fiat is the latest steward of the Jeep brand: the brand that saved Willys, saved Kaiser, saved American Motors and saved Chrysler on more than one occasion. As Yogi Berra, so fondly remembered earlier in this book, said: "It's déjà vu all over again."

Chapter 29
Conflicts of Interest???

The sale of American Motors by Renault to Chrysler had everything a good thriller needed: egos, differing agendas, death, and international intrigue. It was a complex arrangement, structure, and dealt with many of the participants serving multiple roles and constituents. Fiduciary responsibility, long-term financial consequences, concern for staff, and personal issues were all in play. In some instances, fiduciary responsibility was ignored or at least rationalized away. In others, concern for one's own personal interests tilted the scale.

And, finally, the deal had more than enough conflicts of interest, starting with the Renault executives serving as directors on the AMC Board. They were clearly not "independent directors" as they were placed there to oversee and protect Renault's interests. Nothing sinister there on its face, but since board directors of a public company have a fiduciary responsibility for all shareholders, even in a "controlled company," this meant that they had an inherent conflict to begin with – serving two masters.

The true "independent directors" of the AMC Board were less than happy when it was disclosed that their fellow directors from Renault were attending AMC board meetings while at the same time taking part in secret talks between Chrysler and Renault regarding the potential sale of AMC.

Once the public announcement was made, the AMC independent directors quickly met without the Renault-appointed directors. AMC's former-Chairman, Paul Tippett, assumed the lead director role and formed a "special committee" of three directors – himself, Roy Chapin, Jr., and Canadian Ed Lumley – that took as tough a line as was possible during the due diligence period to maximize the benefits to AMC shareholders in their meetings with Chrysler's Ben Bidwell and Steve Miller.

Two of the Renault-appointed AMC directors worked for firms on retainer with Renault, so, in effect, they were being paid for their participation. Those gents were Felix G. Rohatyn of Lazard Investment Bank and Allan M. Chapin of the legal firm Sullivan & Cromwell. In the event of the sale of Renault's interest to Chrysler and the subsequent purchase, by tendering for the balance of the remaining AMC shares, Lazard received "completion fees" as well as their ongoing billings.

Felix Rohatyn was, in fact, the key player behind the Renault/Chrysler transaction. He had important contacts with the leaders at all constituent parties. He also had knowledge of the priorities of these constituents. More important, Rohatyn knew how to approach complex deals, and what worked and what would not. He was an expert at

taking all the inputs and structuring a deal that nobody
would like, but everyone could accept.

But, he was more than that: Rohatyn was the glue. He
had initially introduced Chrysler CEO Lee Iacocca to
Renault Chairman Georges Besse to start the sale process
rolling. He also played a pivotal role throughout the
process, and was heavily involved in the early stages before
Chrysler and Renault started to deal directly with one
another with lesser support by investment bankers and
outside lawyers. Allan Chapin's law firm, Sullivan &
Cromwell, provided all of the legal support and advice for
Renault.

José Dedeurwaerder, the former head of AMC and Joe
Cappy's boss even after he moved back to France, also was
a pivotal player. José was Renault's top negotiator, and
while reporting to Georges Besse, Dedeurwaerder was able
to slow down and almost shut down the talks with Chrysler.
Why? Dedeurwaerder understood the importance of the
U.S. marketplace for a company like Renault, which
needed to compete in the worldwide automotive industry to
stay viable and competitive. (In fact it happened: Renault,
not including its new partner from 1999, Nissan, dropped
from sixth place as a worldwide automotive manufacturer
in 1977 to eleventh place in 2014. The fifth and sixth
largest automotive manufacturers in 2014 built more than
two million more vehicles each than Renault).

Dedeurwaerder also knew that AMC had turned the corner on large operating losses and was in a strong profit swing, thanks mostly to the current and upcoming Jeep vehicles.

Again, the independent AMC directors were ticked about how Renault's appointed directors were attending AMC board meetings, yet taking part in secret talks between Chrysler and Renault, and not disclosing that fact to their fellow AMC board members.

They could understand how Dedeurwaerder, being a Renault employee, could participate in such talks, but couldn't believe that Felix Rohatyn and Allan Chapin could continue to attend AMC board meetings while actively involved in secret negotiating roles on behalf of Renault with Chrysler. How can one person represent the "best interests" of each of many different constituents?

A conflict of interest? To many of the AMC directors it was mind boggling that Felix Rohatyn not only was engaged as a Renault advisor and a member of the AMC board, while at the same time, an active sales agent on Chrysler's behalf, attempting to assist Chrysler in buying AMC from his client. Finally, if successful on a sale to Chrysler, his firm Lazard would receive a significant fee as a financial advisor for the sale. Basically, Rohatyn could hardly lose, since he was on all sides of the deal!

The July 1987 proxy covering the proposed merger between Chrysler and American Motors said it all: "AMC has been advised that...Lazard has been retained by Renault to render banking advice in connection with Renault's sale of its interest in AMC for a fee payable in the event the merger is consummated."

With that, Felix Rohatyn officially became the key man behind the scenes with both a retainer and success fee, all-the-while sitting on the AMC board as a director. It was akin to a married couple considering divorce using the same attorney.

Allan Chapin also profited handsomely, since Renault, which placed him on the AMC board, engaged his law firm to be their legal advisor. Chapin – no relation to independent board member Roy Chapin, Jr. – handled all of the legal work on the sale to Chrysler, the biggest merger in automotive history at the time, and a huge pay day for his law firm.

After the Besse assassination and the appointment of the new CEO Raymond Levy, Renault's José Dedeurwaerder was unable to slow down or impede the process of the talks between Renault and Chrysler. His futile attempt to secure a key executive position at Chrysler by directly approaching Lee Iacocca, however, may have swayed his actions in the final negotiations with Chrysler. It is interesting to speculate whether Dedeurwaerder could have stopped the deal if Georges Besse had not have been gunned down.

Joe Cappy also had an important role in keeping AMC functioning during the months-long due diligence period. Cappy walked a tightrope. He enjoyed his CEO role, yet realized that if Chrysler's acquisition was successful, his position would be eliminated. But due to his contact and relationship with Chrysler's Ben Bidwell, he felt comfortable that there would be a good position for him at Chrysler if the deal indeed closed.

Since Renault had announced its intention to stop funding American Motors if the deal cratered, Cappy knew AMC was at the end of its rope. At times, Cappy wasn't certain which side he was on.

American Motors' independent members of its board of directors, along with their financial and legal advisors, armed with tons of analyses, finally concluded that the price Chrysler was offering AMC shareholders was a "fair value" if their offer of $4.25 per share was raised to $4.50. AMC couldn't continue to operate for long without Renault's financial support. After further discussion and much debate, Chrysler agreed and the $4.50 per share offer was endorsed by the AMC Board and accepted by the shareholders.

Could the AMC shareholders have gotten a better deal had Rohatyn and Chapin recused themselves from the AMC board once the secret talks began? No one will ever know. Once the agreement between Renault and Chrysler was publicly announced, however, the AMC independent directors held the balance of the AMC board meetings without the Renault-appointed directors.

Shearson Lehman Brothers, the AMC board's financial advisor issued a one-page "fairness" letter, blessed the deal, and took home a $3.5 million check. As they say, when the buffet table is laid out, get out of the way of the hogs or get trampled.

Chapter 30
Epilogue by Joe Cappy

Let's see, 26 years with Ford Motor Company, five years with American Motors Corporation, ten years with Chrysler Corporation, six years with Dollar Thrifty Automotive Group: that's 47 years of corporate life. I've enjoyed every day – some more than others, of course. The sun doesn't always shine, but you learn a lot when adversity strikes as well.

Over those 47 years, I was fortunate to have some very responsible positions. Yet, in looking back over the years, there were many assignments that I enjoyed equally as well as the senior positions. At the time, each job I was in seemed to be my favorite. I enjoyed them all and the people I worked with and for. I was excited to go to work every day. It wasn't the position or the money—it was the feeling of accomplishment in helping the company be successful.

Some memorable positions still bring a smile to my face. My assignment as a Dealer Auditor at Ford Motor, and then as Dealer Audit Supervisor, were great springboards for visibility within the Ford Motor Company. Then, as an analyst in Sales Analysis, I was convinced that I would rather be a pitcher than a catcher, since I believed I could develop marketing programs that were better than those I was requested to "cost-out" by the marketing people

– that is why I asked to be transferred to marketing from finance.

My first marketing assignment at Ford was at Marketing Staff working for Norman Krandall and Jacques Maroni, and it was exhilarating. I was one of about ten young, bright fellows who believed we were going to jump-start Ford's business around the world. The assignment brought international travel and the opportunity to meet high quality people working in Ford's overseas operations like future CEO Alex Trotman at Ford of England. The results of this study group were warmly received with many of the recommendations acted upon by senior Ford management over the next several years.

My first tour of duty at Ford Division resulted from Norman Krandall taking me along when he went there as Marketing Plans Manager and named me Light Truck Marketing Plans Manager. This assignment brought me into contact with key executives in light truck sales, marketing, advertising, product planning, and engineering. The joint efforts of this key group of people allowed Ford Motor to reclaim light truck leadership from Chevrolet for the first time in 33 years – a position Ford still proudly holds today.

At that time, I also reported to or worked under John Naughton and Phillip Caldwell, both of whom had very high standards of excellence. And, I saw in action a man I met in Cleveland when he was the District Sales Manager and I was a dealer auditor, Gordon MacKenzie. MacKenzie would play a huge part in my career. He was the most enthusiastic and optimistic executive I'd ever met. He was beloved by the dealer body and the field sales force.

With advice and counsel from MacKenzie and Geoff Curran, I requested a special developmental assignment as a field sales manager in the Detroit District calling on dealers on the east side of Detroit, and extending into southern Ohio. This position taught me how to beg, plead, and grovel, and use "float" to sell my allotment of wholesale vehicles each month – and then assist the dealers in turning them into retail sales and RDCs (retail delivery cards).

Next followed an assignment with recreational vehicles and an ill-fated effort to build a product Ford Motor had no experience or business in doing so.

Let's fast forward here, when I was sent back to Ford's HQ – The Glass House – and the Marketing Staff, working for Grant Chave. My mentors, MacKenzie and Curran convinced me to take another developmental assignment. This time as Louisville District Sales Manager, with responsibility for 154 Ford dealers in Kentucky, southern Indiana, and eastern Tennessee. It would prove to be one of my favorite assignments. To be in charge of a sales staff and dealers and responsible for their performance versus the competitors and other districts was very fulfilling. My two top assistants in Louisville, Bob Garrett and Jim

Galvin, handled all of the administrative and personnel matters, which allowed me to be the relationship fellow and visit all 154 dealerships at their place of business to strengthen their ties with Ford. This assignment allowed me to develop strategy and a culture of teamwork with a group of people that was invaluable later in my career. It also provided me with strong friendships that are thankfully still in place today.

Gordon MacKenzie brought me back to Dearborn, Michigan, where I was named General Marketing Manager for Lincoln-Mercury Division. It was exciting to work for MacKenzie. He was always enthusiastic – except on one occasion, when everything was going wrong and it didn't appear that there was any solution to the problems facing Gordon's team. Gordon looked depressed, but he started talking and waving his arms around until he became upbeat, and after more talk and more arm waving, he had his entire staff charged up and ready to go back into action.

A headhunter contacted me about an officer level position at American Motors Corporation. I agreed to be interviewed, if only to test the market of my value. Gerald Meyers, Chairman and CEO, and Paul Tippett, President and COO, interviewed me. I knew and liked Tippett from my knowledge of him at Ford. After the interview there was no immediate feedback from the headhunter or AMC. Weeks passed without word. I was curious with the silent treatment, so I finally contacted the headhunter to find out why I had not heard back from anyone. I was told that the delay had nothing to do with me, but involved some internal issues.

In January 1982, Gerald Meyers resigned and Paul Tippett replaced Meyers as Chairman and CEO. Replacing Tippett as President was a Renault appointee, José Dedeurwaerder, who had been in charge of AMC's Manufacturing and Product Development. The headhunter soon called, requesting I return for another set of interviews with the new senior management team. The Tippett interview was perfunctory since we had already gone through the process. The interview with José Dedeurwaerder was breathtaking. He appeared to me to be a combination of Lee Iacocca and Gordon MacKenzie all rolled into one. He also laid out for me Renault's control of AMC and how Renault was a Crown Corporation of the French Government. In answer to my question regarding the long-term viability of AMC, he pointed out that the French Treasury provided the financial backing for the Company. An offer soon followed the interview and I was hooked.

My complete AMC experience has been detailed in the chapters of this book. It was the experience of a lifetime, and one I would repeat in a heartbeat. Especially beginning in 1985, which John Tierney called, "The best of times, the worst of times" (Detroit and Paris, not London and Paris, my apologies to Charles Dickens). AMC's operations were trimmed out, the Renault Alliance was introduced, the Jeep XJ Cherokee was continuing to ramp up in sales volume, and everything was beginning to run smoothly.

Unfortunately, Renault, our "sugar daddy," was facing difficult situations in France with Georges Besse's efforts at restructuring Renault. In addition, the French workweek had been had been cut from 40 hours to 35 hours with the same pay. This required Renault to be at 90 percent of capacity to just breakeven profit-wise. During the 1981-1986 period, the mothership Renault lost about six billion French francs. While AMC losses in this period accounted for less than 10 percent of Renault's total global loss, it was perceived as a drag on the parent company and was constantly highlighted by the French media and politicians. At this point of the book, you know how these factors impacted AMC's fate.

After the acquisition of American Motors by Chrysler, I was given several assignments, including leading Chrysler's International Operations, which involved heavy travel around the world meeting an elite group of distributors who headed up vehicle distribution in their own countries by establishing a network of retail outlets and parts warehouses. Also, there were a number of countries where Chrysler took over AMC's overseas operations assembling Jeep vehicles from boxed kits (CKD or Complete Knock Down: think the model car you as a kid built out of a box, only a real, full-size vehicle) in China,

Egypt, Venezuela and Israel. We also started an assembly partnership with Styer AG in Graz, Austria, for production of Chrysler's groundbreaking minivans.

During this time, interestingly, Chrysler explored a possible alliance with Fiat. This was the second time I was involved with a possible tie-in with the Italian automaker. My first was in 1967 when Henry Ford II and Gianni Agnelli, Fiat's Chairman, were interested in discussing a deal, but Ford couldn't find one of his vice presidents willing to undertake the assignment.

The Chrysler study involved a number of possibilities for joint ventures. Toward the end of these studies, I was in Turin with other Chrysler vice presidents where we previewed future Fiat products. We were quartered in Fiat's famous guest Villa. After dinner we walked out on the patio to enjoy the night air. I mentioned to my peers to enjoy the moment, since regardless how the present negotiations turned out, this would likely be the last time we would be allowed to enjoy Fiat's Villa. Nothing came of these discussions, and as far as I am aware, that was the last time the Villa hosted a Chrysler executive.

After several years heading up Chrysler's International Operations, I was asked to divest six non-core businesses that Chrysler owned. This followed a strategy meeting led by new CEO Bob Eaton and all of the senior officers to determine what the company's focus should be going forward. The answer was actually simple: develop, manufacture, and sell cars and trucks, and shed businesses we didn't understand or could not manage properly.

An aerospace company, a security communication company (think "Homeland Security"), and a tank weapons system company were all profitable and relatively easy to sell. The remaining three rental car companies Chrysler owned, headquartered in Tulsa, Oklahoma, were losing a combined $5 million a month. No one is interested in buying unprofitable companies – even if given to them for free. I requested Bob Eaton to relocate my wife Patty and me to Tulsa, with a "get-out-of-jail-free" card providing us, after the sale of the companies, with paid relocation to any place in the continental United States.

My time in Tulsa was most fulfilling and provided me with experiences that were the equivalent of a PhD in business, and allowed me to use all of the skills I had learned along the way from Ford to AMC to Chrysler. I had some outstanding assistants to help make dramatic changes to these companies like Jeff Higgs, Don Himelfarb, Gary Paxton, Ron Elder, Steve Hildebrand, Pete Kauchek, and Peter Guptill.

One rental car company, Snappy Car Rental, that operated at breakeven or a slight profit, was sold to a financial group in New York City. That left Dollar Rent-A-Car and Thrifty Car Rental for my team to return to profitability. Dollar was the big challenge. Dollar was actually bankrupt when it was purchased by Chrysler and was hampered by split operations in Los Angeles and Tulsa, and a semi-independent operator controlling the State of Florida, who ran the operation in a manner to maximize his own personal income, not the company's.

Even after Dollar and Thrifty were brought under control, potential buyers were skeptical that the improvements in performance were permanent. Presentations were made to Hertz, Avis, and AutoNation without success, some more than once. I then went to the Chrysler board in September 1997 for approval to attempt to take the two companies public in an IPO venture. By that time the two companies had been merged into one organization. With the assistance of Credit Suisse First Boston, we arranged road trips to meet with potential investors in Europe, Japan, and the large cities in the United States. The IPO was very successful with Chrysler getting a handsome payday of $450 million and DollarThrifty Automotive Group being listed on the New York Stock Exchange (NYSE: DTG) at the end of December 1997. I assumed the position of Chairman, CEO and President.

For the full year of 1998, and through mid-year 2001, DTG reported the highest return on sales versus its competitors. The roof fell in on September 11, 2001, when terrorists smashed commercial airplanes into the World Trade Center. For the first time ever, all air travel was grounded for three days. With this act of terrorism, our world changed. Renters of cars with keys in their hands drove to their homes wherever they lived. Rental cars were dispersed and scattered all over the country, as though hit by a tornado or hurricane.

In response, DTG, realizing that the entire travel industry was going to be negatively impacted beyond anyone's imagination, took action to reduce its fleet by 20 percent in less than 60 days, put into effect a 20 percent reduction in workforce, and requested all mid-level and senior executives take a ten- to 25-percent reduction in salary, based upon their classification on a sliding schedule, with no bonuses, but with an earn-back feature if certain profit levels were achieved. The DTG board had a problem with an earn-back feature, and setting bonus targets below prior year profit levels.

As CEO, I refused to budge and argued fiercely with the board over our plan to combat the disaster facing air travel. Two of the directors who knew me well came into my office and wanted to talk with me in private. I told them – point blank – that they could either remove me, or I would quit if they didn't approve our disaster recovery plan.

One characteristic ingrained in me as a youngster, can be viewed as either a plus or minus, yet it remains with me today. If I believe I am right, I will never back-off until I am told to "shut up and don't bring it up again!" Even then, I always had to be careful not to pop off again. This trait can be labeled stubbornness, but I prefer to view it as a ***perseverance, coupled with strong confidence*** forged in adversity.

The DTG board finally approved our disaster recovery plan and the company worked hard to close out the year, sailing into the first quarter of 2002 with record profits while <u>all</u> of our competitors lost money. DTG achieved the revised profit targets and all affected employees earned back their salary cuts, while those on the bonus roll received bonuses. The morale of the company was sky-high and we never lost a single employee we wanted to keep.

The moral from this incident, from my perspective, is if your management team strongly supports a plan they develop without board input, the CEO would be a fool not to fight tooth and nail to give them the tools necessary to achieve their goals.

Values and characteristics necessary for success will vary from person to person, based upon the individual's own personality and talents. A trait essential for success and one that I proudly exhibited was ***reliability***. I could always be counted on to accept an assignment and carry it out to completion in a first-class fashion – thanks in great measure to a strong work ethic inherited from my father.

I also had ***"team smarts,"*** the ability to work with others and to mobilize people who were not direct reports. This was possible due to a simple mindset: the ability to be ***concise with sharp focus*** when leading people that allows others to understand and achieve the goals necessary to be successful. It also helps to have great *curiosity* to learn more, and a ***willingness to take risks*** without fear.

Quite frankly, I was rarely the smartest person in the room; but I <u>was</u> the best student.

My career and the history of how AMC came to be, how I got there, what it was like to be "the last CEO of American Motors," and what followed has been detailed in the chapters of this book with Jason Vines, who went from being my young PR guy and speechwriter at Chrysler, to being a great friend with tons of stories on his own about the rough and tumble world of the international auto industry. When his first book came out in 2014, I was quickly on the phone to him: "We've gotta tell my story, Jason."

Well, that's 47 years of corporate life. Reflecting back on my career has been an incredible and enjoyable experience. It was quite a ride and one I would do over without hesitation. I had a ball!

Acknowledgments

When you tell a real-life story that encompasses 100 years, you have a lot of people to thank for making the story possible, and making this book a reality. It is our hope that the men and women who had a hand in creating what eventually became American Motors, accept this book as a testament to their hard work and courage and to honor the memory of those no longer with us.

As relayed in this book, Joe Cappy said he was never the smartest guy in the room, but he was the best student. He beams with pride that he was able to bring with him 100 of his top executives at American Motors after Chrysler's acquisition. Many of them soared in the new company. They included Tim Adams, Freda Bane, Jackie Beckman, Francois Castaing, Joe ChamaSrour, Tom Drauer, Rich Everett, Rex Franson, Dan Glinecki, Bill Grabowski, Pete Grady, Steve Harris, Gene Heidemann, Jon Holcomb, Rick Houtman, Terry Houtman, Jim Issner, Jim Julow, John Kent, Marty Levine, Bob Longstreth, Rita McKay, John Miller, Dennis Montone, Kathy Murrenus, Mike Yatsko, John Russell, Chris Theodore, John Tierney, Jeff Trimmer, Don St. Pierre, Bob Williams, Craig Winn, Frank Yaconis and many others.

The men and women of the Ford Motor Company were a huge, early, positive influence on Joe Cappy's career, life, work ethic and character. Meanwhile, Lee Iacocca's brilliant vision is the major reason Jeep was able to soar to even greater heights under Chrysler ownership.

To put this book together took tenacity, long nights of research and writing, pride, and knocking out a few cob webs in the memory bank by Joe and me.

It also took the collective memory of many people vital in this story – Jim Donlan, Ralph Sarotte, Pete Guptill, Joe ChamaShour, Jerry Sloan, Steve Harris, John Tierney, Francois Castaing, Dick Calmes and Craig Harper. Plus, a huge shout-out to Gerard Gastaut and his encyclopedic brilliance of Renault and AMC's history and his website, www.historierenault.net.

And, most important, it took patience, support and an occasional back rub, along with rum and vodka, from our wives – Patty Cappy and Betsy Vines – to get it over the goal line.

A very special "thank you" to our alma mater, Chrysler (now FCA) for giving us access to their wonderful archives and cost-free use of the fabulous photographs in this book. Grazie Gualberto Ranieri and Brandt Rosenbusch!

Finally, thank you for all the hard work editing – Carol McCrow, Holly Park and Michelle Morrow – and publishing – Barbara Terry – this book.

Author Bios
Jason Vines

Jason Vines, 56, is an independent communications consultant and author. In late 2014 Waldorf Publishing released his first book, *What Did Jesus Drive? – Crisis PR in Cars, Computers and Christianity,* to critical acclaim. Vines followed that with the hilarious compilation of his satirical posts on the Detroit News' political website in *Jimmy Hoffa Called My Mom a Bitch! Profiles in Stupidity* in 2015.

Vines served as the top communications professional for three automakers – Nissan North America, Ford Motor Company, and Chrysler Group between 1998 and 2007. He was named "Top PR Professional" in the automotive industry in 1999, 2005, and 2006 by *Automotive News*, the auto industry's lead trade publication. He is credited with leading some of the most memorable product launches in the automotive industry including the Chrysler 300, Jeep Grand Cherokee, Dodge Viper, and the reborn Nissan 350Z. Vines also was the communications chief during some of the biggest crises in automotive history, including claims of sudden unintended acceleration in Jeep vehicles, kids getting killed by front-seat air bags, a Nissan Motor Corporation on the brink of bankruptcy and, then, perhaps the granddaddy of all business crises, the Ford/Firestone tire crisis in 2000 and 2001.

Vines is Director-Emeritus of the Automotive Hall of Fame, an organization he served as Chairman for two years, and one he hopes to be inducted in someday. But, he is not holding his breath. (Actually he is, as you basically have to be dead to get inducted.)

Vines received a Master's Degree in Labor and Industrial Relations from Michigan State University in 1984 and a B.A. with a double major in Economics and Communications/Theater from Central College in Pella, Iowa in 1982. He has been married to his wife Betsy for more than 29 years and has three college graduates that thankfully are employed and have their own health insurance, cell phone contracts and auto insurance policies. They live in Wilmington, North Carolina and Lewiston, Michigan (Yes, like the Clintons, they have more than one home despite earlier being "dead broke").

Joseph (Joe) E. Cappy

Joseph E. Cappy, 82, was the last President and Chief Executive Officer of American Motors Corporation before the company was acquired by Chrysler Corporation in 1987.

After graduating from the University of Wisconsin with degrees in Accounting and Marketing, Cappy began his automotive career with the Ford Motor Company, first serving as an accountant in the infamous Edsel Division. Over the next 26 years, Cappy would serve in a variety of management functions at Ford, culminating in his appointment as General Marketing Manager of the Lincoln/Mercury Division.

In 1982, the country's smallest major automaker, American Motors, wooed Cappy away from Ford and named him Vice President of the Marketing Group. After accepting increasing levels of responsibility over the next few years and joining the Board of Directors, he was appointed as President and CEO four short years after joining AMC.

Under Cappy's leadership, American Motors changed the entire automotive landscape with the introduction of the 1984 Jeep Cherokee, a compact SUV that took the market by storm. Cappy also oversaw the development and launch of what most consider the quintessential Jeep, the Wrangler, a descendent of original World War II military Jeep.

Upon Chrysler's acquisition of American Motors on August 7, 1987, Cappy was named Vice President of the newly formed Jeep/Eagle Division. He was later named Vice President of Brand Development, then Vice President of International Operations, and finally, Vice President of Chrysler Technologies and Rental Car Operations, with the responsibility to spin-off those operations considered non-core essential to the automaker.

In 1998, Cappy was appointed CEO, Director and President of the DollarThrifty Group, where he spun Dollar Rent a Car and Thrifty Car Rental from Chrysler in a successful IPO and placed the merged companies as a newly independent company on the New York Stock Exchange under the symbol NYSE: DTG. Cappy retired in 2003 after leading DTG to a strong position in the rental car industry as the value leader. Hertz acquired DTG in November 2012.

Joe Cappy lives with his wife Patty in their homes in Harbor Springs, Michigan, and Tulsa, Oklahoma.

Cappy served his country as a 2nd Lieutenant in the U.S. Army Reserves, and retired as a Captain.

Footnotes

1) Hyde, Charles K., *Storied Independent Automakers: Nash, Hudson and American Motors*, page 35, Wayne State University Press, November 2009. (All Hyde quotes used with permission from Mr. Hyde and Wayne State University Press.)

2) Hyde, Charles K., *Storied Independent Automakers: Nash, Hudson and American Motors*, page 37, Wayne State University Press, November 2009.

3) Hyde, Charles K., *Storied Independent Automakers: Nash, Hudson and American Motors*, page 42, Wayne State University Press, November 2009.

4) Hyde, Charles K., *Storied Independent Automakers: Nash, Hudson and American Motors*, page 51, Wayne State University Press, November 2009.

5) Hyde, Charles K., *Storied Independent Automakers: Nash, Hudson and American Motors*, page 51, Wayne State University Press, November 2009.

6) Hyde, Charles K., *Storied Independent Automakers: Nash, Hudson and American Motors*, page 76, Wayne State University Press, November 2009.

7) Foster, Patrick R., *American Motors: The Last Independent*, page 8, Krause Publications, March 1993. (Mr. Foster, who holds arguably the most extensive collection of American Motors, and it predecessor companies' memorabilia and photography, gave us permission to use his quote in this book.)

Reference Pages